ANNOTATED BIBLIOGRAPHY OF FILMS IN AUTOMATION, DATA PROCESSING, AND COMPUTER SCIENCE

ANNOTATED BIBLIOGRAPHY OF FILMS IN AUTOMATION, DATA PROCESSING, AND COMPUTER SCIENCE

Martin B. Solomon, Jr.

and

Nora Geraldine Lovan

University of Kentucky Press

1967

PREFACE

This annotated bibliography of motion pictures related to automation, data processing, and computer science lists all films of this nature that we we were able to locate. Films peripheral to these subjects have also been included in an attempt at completeness. Nevertheless, we acknowledge that many films may have been omitted because of our ignorance of their existence.

An explanation of each part of this compilation is in order.

The *Index of Titles* is an alphabetical listing that gives the code number used for each film in the numerically arranged Annotated Bibliography.

The *Index of Subjects* is a permutation of a number of keywords chosen to depict the contents of each film. Each subject is listed once to the right of the center space of the column, and the associated film code which links the subject to the Annotated Bibliography is shown at the right. For example, if you want to locate a film dealing with the effects of automation on labor and society in general, you will find under LABOR references to a number of films. The third entry reads:

LABOR MANAGEMENT SOCIETY=   F0128

This film appears to cover the subjects you are interested in, and so you would look for the code F0128 in the Annotated Bibliography for a fuller description. The same film can also be found under the keywords AUTOMATION, MANAGEMENT, and SOCIETY.

In the *Annotated Bibliography of Films*, the first line of each description includes the film code, the year of production, and an indicator that specifies the type of audience for which the film seems appropriate:

A—adult   B—professional   C—college
J—juvenile   S—senior high school

The second line is the title of the film. Then follows a short section which gives information about who produced the film, who released it, and where it may be purchased if it is for sale. A second paragraph describes the film briefly. Next listed are four attributes of the film: viewing time, sound (SD.) or silent (SL.), color or black and white (B/W), and projector size. Last is the ordering information for borrowing film: the name of the organization from which the film may be borrowed, the charge if any, and special instructions. For most films, the title should be specified when ordering; this is indicated by NAME. When a number or a code is required, this is listed.

The *Directory of Film Depositories* gives full addresses for the organizations mentioned in the Annotated Bibliography and, in some cases, additional information about deadlines, prices, and other policies of the depository.

Acknowledgments

The information contained in the compilation was gathered from many sources. Thanks are due especially to the Washington, D.C., chapter of the Association for Computing Machinery, whose groundwork provided the incentive and the beginning for this project.

We greatly appreciate the aid of the University of Kentucky Computing Center, which graciously provided the necessary support for the project.

Lexington, Kentucky   M. B. S., Jr.
June, 1967   N. G. L.

ANNOTATED BIBLIOGRAPHY OF FILMS IN AUTOMATION, DATA PROCESSING, AND COMPUTER SCIENCE

INDEX OF TITLES

IMAGE-PROCESSING= F0099
COMPUTERS INDUSTRIAL-PROCESS-CONTROL= F0116
COMPUTERS INDUSTRIAL-PROCESS-CONTROL= F0185
AUTOMATION INDUSTRY BENEFITS PROBLEMS= F0018
ION ELECTRONIC EQUIPMENT INDUSTRY BENEFITS= AUTOMAT F0025
ELECTRONICS INDUSTRY COMPUTERS TRANSISTORS= F0002
OMPUTERS DATA-PROCESSING INDUSTRY FAR-EAST= C F0157
COMPUTERS PETROLEUM INDUSTRY ON-LINE= F0102
AL-SECURITY= COMPUTERS INDUSTRY PETROLEUM MACHINE-TOOLS SOCI F0104
OMATION LABOR MANAGEMENT INDUSTRY POLITICS= AUT F0011
ELECTRONICS INDUSTRY PRODUCTS RAYTHEON-HISTORY= F0010
COMPUTERS AEROSPACE INDUSTRY REAL-TIME FLIGHT SIMULATION= F0165
ANALOG-COMPUTERS ON-LINE INDUSTRY SIMULATION= F0229
AUTOMATION INDUSTRY= F0039
AUTOMATION INDUSTRY= F0156
AUTOMATION EGG INDUSTRY= F0042
AUTOMATION EGG INDUSTRY= F0164
ATH-20 NUMERICAL-CONTROL INDUSTRY= COMPUTERS DYNAP F0203
710 ON-LINE PAPER-MAKING INDUSTRY= COMPUTERS IBM-1 F0080
PROCESSING MOTOR-FREIGHT INDUSTRY= COMPUTERS IBM-1401 DATA- F0069
INFORMATION STORAGE-DEVICES DISKS= F0071
TAPES= INFORMATION STORAGE-DEVICES MAGNETIC F0075
COMPUTERS INFORMATION STORAGE-DEVICES= F0053
COMMUNICATION= INFORMATION-RETRIEVAL DATA-PROCESSING F0073
ATURE-RESEARCH-SYSTEM= INFORMATION-RETRIEVAL TECHNICAL-LITER F0024
INFORMATION-RETRIEVAL= F0236
NSE-DOCUMENTATION-CENTER INFORMATION-RETRIEVAL= ASTIA DEFE F0038
COMPUTERS INSURANCE INFORMATION-SYSTEM= F0212
SELECTIVE DISSEMINATION INFORMATION= F0086
DATA-PROCESSING INPUT OUTPUT STORAGE-DEVICES= F0094
TERS NCR-390 SOLID-STATE INPUT OUTPUT= COMPU F0078
TROL MACHINE-TOOLS PAPER INPUT-CONTROL TAPE= NUMERICAL-CON F0001
COMPUTER-ORIENTED INSTRUCTION= F0085
TE-INQUIRY= COMPUTERS INSURANCE IBM-1014 RANDOM-ACCESS REMO F0120
COMPUTERS INSURANCE INFORMATION-SYSTEM= F0212
MONOLITHIC INTEGRATED CIRCUITRY= F0191
RELATIONSHIP= COMPUTERS INTRODUCTION ANALOG DIGITAL= F0108
FEEDBACK INTRODUCTION MATHEMATICS MAN-MACHINE- F0121
PROGRAMMING INTRODUCTION= F0050
COMPUTERS INTRODUCTION= F0027
INVENTORY= F0054
COMPUTERS SPACE JOHN-GLENN-FLIGHT= F0115
AUTOMATION LABOR BENEFITS PROBLEMS= F0056
AUTOMATION LABOR MANAGEMENT INDUSTRY POLITICS= F0011
AUTOMATION LABOR MANAGEMENT SOCIETY= F0128
AUTOMATION LABOR PROBLEMS= F0180
AUTOMATION SKILLED LABOR PROBLEMS= F0032
AUTOMATION LABOR= F0210
ISTORY BENEFITS PROBLEMS LABOR= AUTOMATION H F0204
CATIONS BENEFITS SKILLED LABOR= AUTOMATION DEFINITION APPLI F0016
COMPUTERS LANGUAGE AUTOPROMPT= F0066
COMPUTERS LANGUAGE LIGHT-PEN-DRAWING TX-2= F0127
COMPUTERS TX-2 LANGUAGE LIGHT-PEN-DRAWING= F0161
L MACHINE-TOOLS= APT LANGUAGE PROGRAMMING NUMERICAL-CONTRO F0221
COMPUTERS LANGUAGE= F0130
PROGRAMMING FORTRAN-IV LANGUAGE= F0243
COMPUTERS LANGUAGES AD APT AUTOSPOT= F0160
COMPUTERS PROGRAMMING LANGUAGES= F0202
COMPUTERS IBM LASER= F0151
COMPUTERS APPLICATIONS LATIN AMERICA= F0227
ESSING ECONOMY EDUCATION LATIN-AMERICA= COMPUTERS DATA-PROC F0177
HUMAN LEARNING BEHAVIOR= F0051
PROGRAMMED LEARNING= F0217
PERT LESS U.S.-NAVY= F0067
S= COMPUTERS LGP-30 PROGRAMMING CIRCUITS FLOWCHART F0049
COMPUTERS LANGUAGE LIGHT-PEN-DRAWING TX-2= F0127
COMPUTERS TX-2 LANGUAGE LIGHT-PEN-DRAWING= F0161
COMPUTERS LOGIC-ELEMENTS= F0109
COMPUTERS LOGIC-SYMBOLS= F0110
ROCESSING U.S.-AIR-FORCE LOGISTIC-SUPPORT MANAGEMENT= DATA-P F0215
SIMULATION LUNAR-LANDING= F0230
E= NUMERICAL-CONTROL MACHINE-TOOLS PAPER INPUT-CONTROL TAP F0001
UTERS INDUSTRY PETROLEUM MACHINE-TOOLS SOCIAL-SECURITY= COMP F0104
NUMERICAL-CONTROL MACHINE-TOOLS= F0022
AMMING NUMERICAL-CONTROL MACHINE-TOOLS= APT LANGUAGE PROGR F0221
AUTOMATIC MACHINES RELIABILITY= F0200
MACHINES= F0006
AGEMENT-CONTROL BUSINESS MACHINES= ELECTRONIC DATA-PROCESSING F0013
COMPUTERS MAGNETIC CARD MEMORY= F0206
MAGNETIC TAPES MANUFACTURE= F0192
MAGNETIC TAPES= F0020
ORMATION STORAGE-DEVICES MAGNETIC TAPES= INF F0075
MAN-MACHINE-RELATIONSHIP= F0113
INTRODUCTION MATHEMATICS MAN-MACHINE-RELATIONSHIP= COMPUTERS F0121
MAN-MACHINE-RELATIONSHIPS= F0149
AUTOMATION LABOR MANAGEMENT INDUSTRY POLITICS= F0011
AUTOMATION LABOR MANAGEMENT SOCIETY= F0128
ECTRONIC DATA-PROCESSING MANAGEMENT-CONTROL BUSINESS MACHINES= F0013
COMPUTERS MANAGEMENT= F0201
COMPUTERS IBM-1440 MANAGEMENT= F0150
R-FORCE LOGISTIC-SUPPORT MANAGEMENT= DATA-PROCESSING U.S.-AI F0215
NONNUMERICAL MANIPULATION SYMBOLS= F0240
PRINTED-CIRCUITS MANUFACTURE REPAIR= F0081
MAGNETIC TAPES MANUFACTURE= F0192
AUTOMATION-EQUIPMENT MANUFACTURE= F0139
DATAPLOTTER MAPS CHARTS= F0199
COMPUTERS MARKETING= F0183
I-1627 IBM-1620 DRAFTING MATERIAL-PROCESS= COMPUTERS IBM-140 F0158
ES= AUTOMATED-MACHINES MATERIALS-HANDLING FACTORIES WAREHOUS F0034
ION= COMPUTERS MATHEMATICAL-MODELS DISIGNING SIMULAT F0122
COMPUTERS BINARY MATHEMATICS COUNTING-SYSTEMS= F0035
S= BINARY MATHEMATICS DIGITAL COMPUTERS BUSINES F0009
COMPUTERS INTRODUCTION MATHEMATICS MAN-MACHINE-RELATIONSHIP= F0121
MATHEMATICS RANDOM-EVENTS= F0126
MATHEMATICS-ASPECTS= F0076
MATHEMATICS-FANTASY= F0041
MATHEMATICS= F0068
MATHEMATICS= F0116
BINARY MATHEMATICS= F0218
COMPUTERS HIGH-SCHOOL MATHEMATICS= F0072
TION APPLICATIONS BINARY MATHEMATICS= COMPUTERS OPERA F0072
ANCY SYMBOLS TIME BINARY MATHEMATICS= COMMUNICATION REDUND F0000
SUPERCONDUCTIVITY MEMORY-PLANE-PRODUCTION= F0088
COMPUTERS MAGNETIC CARD MEMORY= F0206
SPACE TRACKING-STATIONS MERCURY-PROJECT= COMPUTERS F0093
ELECTRONICS MILITARY AIRBORNE AUTOMATION= F0033

COMPUTERS MILITARY U.S.-ARMY MOBIDIC= F0123
COMPUTERS MISSILES AIR-DEFENSE= F0044
UTERS MILITARY U.S.-ARMY MOBIDIC= COMP F0123
MONOLITHIC INTEGRATED CIRCUITRY= F0191
IBM-1401 DATA-PROCESSING MOTOR-FREIGHT INDUSTRY= COMPUTERS F0069
COMPUTERS MOVIES= F0211
MPUTERS ANIMATED-DIAGRAM MOVIES= CO F0182
COMPUTERS MUSIC= F0184
COMPUTERS U.S.-AIR-FORCE NASA= X-15 ROCKETS AIRPLANES F0046
ATA-PROCESSING COMPUTERS NCR-315= D F0219
COMPUTERS NCR-390 SOLID-STATE INPUT OUTPUT= F0078
NONNUMERICAL MANIPULATION SYMBOLS= F0240
COMPUTERS NUMERICAL-CONTROL DESIGN-AUTOMATION= F0105
COMPUTERS DYNAPATH-20 NUMERICAL-CONTROL INDUSTRY= F0203
INPUT-CONTROL TAPE NUMERICAL-CONTROL MACHINE-TOOLS PAPER F0001
NUMERICAL-CONTROL MACHINE-TOOLS= F0022
APT LANGUAGE PROGRAMMING NUMERICAL-CONTROL MACHINE-TOOLS= F0221
AUTOSPOT AUTOMAP NUMERICAL-CONTROL= F0103
COMPUTERS ASTRONOMY OAO= F0124
COMPUTERS OLYMPIC-GAMES= F0145
COMPUTERS OLYMPIC-GAMES= F0061
DATA-PROCESSING OLYMPIC-GAMES= F0237
MPUTERS IBM-1062 FINANCE ON-LINE DATA-PROCESSING= CO F0142
ANALOG-COMPUTERS ON-LINE INDUSTRY SIMULATION= F0229
COMPUTERS IBM-1710 ON-LINE PAPER-MAKING INDUSTRY= F0080
UTERS PETROLEUM INDUSTRY ON-LINE= COMP F0102
OPERATING-SYSTEMS= F0196
TICS= COMPUTERS OPERATION APPLICATIONS BINARY MATHEMA F0072
COMPUTERS OPTICAL-CHARACTER-READING= F0194
COMPUTERS IBM-1428 OPTICAL-CHARACTER-READING= F0134
COMPUTERS IBM-2260 OPTICAL-DISPLAY COMMUNICATIONS= F0213
DATA-PROCESSING INPUT OUTPUT STORAGE-DEVICES= F0094
CR-390 SOLID-STATE INPUT OUTPUT= COMPUTERS N F0078
RNMENT-APPLICATIONS ASIA PACIFIC-AREA= COMPUTERS GOVE F0228
AL-CONTROL MACHINE-TOOLS PAPER INPUT-CONTROL TAPE= NUMERIC F0001
MPUTERS IBM-1710 ON-LINE PAPER-MAKING INDUSTRY= CO F0080
DATA-PROCESSING PAYROLL= F0112
PERT APPLICATIONS PRINCIPLES= F0197
PERT APPLICATIONS= F0187
PERT COST= F0125
PERT LESS U.S.-NAVY= F0067
COMPUTERS PETROLEUM INDUSTRY ON-LINE= F0102
TY= COMPUTERS INDUSTRY PETROLEUM MACHINE-TOOLS SOCIAL-SECURI F0104
COMPUTERS AUTOMATION PHOTOGRAPHIC-TECHNIQUES= F0030
COMPUTERS POLICE COURTS= F0234
ABOR MANAGEMENT INDUSTRY POLITICS= AUTOMATION L F0011
PERT APPLICATIONS PRINCIPLES= F0197
PRINTED-CIRCUITS MANUFACTURE REPAIR= F0081
ATIC ASSEMBLY TELEVISION PRINTED-CIRCUITS= AUTOM F0007
OMATION HISTORY BENEFITS PROBLEMS LABOR= AUT F0204
AUTOMATION LABOR PROBLEMS= F0180
AUTOMATION SKILLED LABOR PROBLEMS= F0032
UTOMATION LABOR BENEFITS PROBLEMS= A F0056
TOMATION SOCIAL ECONOMIC PROBLEMS= AU F0242
MATION INDUSTRY BENEFITS PROBLEMS= AUTO F0018
COMPUTER IBM-360 PRODUCT-CAPABILITIES= F0169
ORS= COMPUTERS PRODUCTION-LINE-CONTROL CARBON-RESIST F0092
AUTOMATION ELECTRONICS PRODUCTION-PROCESSES COMPUTERS= F0014
ELECTRONICS INDUSTRY PRODUCTS RAYTHEON-HISTORY= F0010
REPORT-GENERATING PROGRAM FARGO RPG= F0084
COMPUTERS SURE PROGRAM= F0082
COMPUTERS BALLISTICS PROGRAM= F0119
COMPUTERS IBM-360 RPG PROGRAM= F0170
PROGRAMMED LEARNING= F0217
LOG-COMPUTERS COMPONENTS PROGRAMMING APPLICATIONS= ANA F0147
COMPUTERS LGP-30 PROGRAMMING CIRCUITS FLOWCHARTS= F0049
COMPUTERS PROGRAMMING FLOWCHARTS COMPILING= F0111
PROGRAMMING FORTRAN-IV LANGUAGE= F0243
PROGRAMMING INTRODUCTION= F0027
COMPUTERS PROGRAMMING LANGUAGES= F0202
-TOOLS= APT LANGUAGE PROGRAMMING NUMERICAL-CONTROL MACHINE F0221
PROGRAMMING= F0233
COMPUTERS PROGRAMMING= F0209
COMPUTERS PROGRAMMING= F0070
OMATIC TEACHING-MACHINES PROGRAMMING= AUT F0091
COMPUTERS HUMAN PSYCHOLOGICAL RESEARCH= F0140
COMPUTERS IBM-1401 PUBLIC-UTILITY ACCOUNTING= F0079
COMPUTERS IBM-1710 PUBLIC-UTILITY= F0143
PUNCHED-CARD ACCOUNTING= F0195
COMPUTERS QUALITY TESTING FEEDBACK= F0153
COMPUTERS IBM-1710 QUALITY TESTING= F0214
AUTOMATION RAILROADS= F0238
RAMAC DEVELOPMENT CAPABILITY= F0036
COMPUTERS IBM RAMAC-305 HOSPITAL ACCOUNTING= F0040
CCESS ACCOUNTING CONTROL RAMAC-305-650= COMPUTERS RANDOM-A F0023
COMPUTERS RAND REMOTE-ACCESS= F0190
C-305-650= COMPUTERS RANDOM-ACCESS ACCOUNTING CONTROL RAMA F0023
OMPUTERS STORAGE-DEVICES RANDOM-ACCESS REAL-TIME= C F0186
UTERS INSURANCE IBM-1014 RANDOM-ACCESS REMOTE-INQUIRY= COMP F0120
COMPUTERS RCA-3488 RANDOM-ACCESS= F0175
MATHEMATICS RANDOM-EVENTS= F0126
RONICS INDUSTRY PRODUCTS RAYTHEON-HISTORY= ELECT F0010
RCA-ACTIVITIES= F0181
COMPUTERS RCA-301 CLERICAL-WORK REAL-TIME= F0135
COMPUTERS RCA-3488 RANDOM-ACCESS= F0175
E= COMPUTERS RCA-501 DATA-PROCESSING U.S.-AIR-FORC F0087
UTERS AEROSPACE INDUSTRY REAL-TIME FLIGHT SIMULATION= COMP F0165
RS RCA-301 CLERICAL-WORK REAL-TIME= COMPUTE F0135
GE-DEVICES RANDOM-ACCESS REAL-TIME= COMPUTERS STORA F0186
ATICS= COMMUNICATION REDUNDANCY SYMBOLS TIME BINARY MATHEM F0000
MACHINES RELIABILITY= F0200
COMPUTERS RAND REMOTE-ACCESS= F0190
E IBM-1014 RANDOM-ACCESS REMOTE-INQUIRY= COMPUTERS INSURANC F0120
TED-CIRCUITS MANUFACTURE REPAIR= PRIN F0081
REPORT-GENERATING PROGRAM FARGO RPG= F0084
ELECTRONICS RESEARCH U.S.-AIR-FORCE= F0216
SCIENCE RESEARCH= F0083
TERS HUMAN PSYCHOLOGICAL RESEARCH= COMPU F0140
FORCE NASA= X-15 ROCKETS AIRPLANES COMPUTERS U.S.-AIR- F0046
SPACE ROCKETS APOLLO-PROJECT COMPUTERS= F0152
COMPUTERS ROCKETS ATLAS-MISSILE= F0198
ROCKETS HISTORY SATURN-PROJECT= F0098
ROCKETS SPACE= F0225
COMPUTERS ROCKETS TITAN= F0223

ANNOTATED BIBLIOGRAPHY OF FILMS

F0000   1952   SCA

A COMMUNICATIONS PRIMER

CHARLES EAMES AND RAY EAMES
RELEASED BY CLASSROOM FILM DISTRIBUTORS, 1959
PURCHASE. CLASSROOM FILM DISTRIBUTORS

AN INTRODUCTION TO THE THEORY OF COMMUNICATION. THIS VERY
STIMULATING AND CREATIVE FILM ASSOCIATES DR. CLAUDE
SHANNON'S (MIT) BASIC THEORETICAL COMMUNICATIONS DIAGRAM
(INFORMATION-SELECTOR-TRANSMITTER-CHANNEL-SIGNAL-
TRANSMITTER-CHANNEL-SIGNAL-RECEIVER-SELECTOR-DESTINATION)
TO TODAY'S PRACTICAL COMMUNICATIONS DEVICES. A DISCUSSION
OF REDUNDANCY, SYMBOLS, TIME, AND BINARY MATHEMATICS
IS INCLUDED.

20 MIN., SD., COLOR 16 MM.

IBM   FREE   NAME

F0001   1953   SCA

A NUMERICALLY CONTROLLED MACHINE TOOL

MIT ELECTRONIC SYSTEMS LAB.

A LUCID EXPOSITION OF THE BASIC PRINCIPLES OF NUMERICAL
CONTROL OF MACHINE TOOLS. THE FILM DESCRIBES THE FIRST
NUMERICALLY CONTROLLED MACHINE TOOL, DEVELOPED IN 1952
BY THE MIT SERVOMECHANISMS LAB., UNDER SPONSORSHIP OF THE
U.S.AIR FORCE. THE FILM SHOWS GRAPHICALLY THE DECODING
OF COMMANDS PUNCHED ON PAPER TAPE INTO CONTROL SIGNALS
WHICH ARE APPLIED TO SERVOMECHANISMS WHICH DRIVE THE
AXES OF MACHINE MOTION. THE BASIC STEPS OF MANUAL
PREPARATION OF INPUT-CONTROL ARE ALSO COVERED.

20 MIN., SD., COLOR, 16 MM.

ELECTRONIC SYSTEMS LABORATORY   FREE   NAME

F0002   1954   CA

AMERICA'S RISING NEW GIANT

DEVRY TECHNICAL INSTITUTE

THIS COLOR FILM VIVIDLY DEMONSTRATES HOW AND WHY
ELECTRONICS HAS BECOME ONE OF AMERICA'S MOST PROMISING
FIELDS OF OPPORTUNITY. INTEREST-GRIPPING SEQUENCES
SHOW HOW ELECTRONICS IS NOW BEING USED IN INDUSTRY
AFTER INDUSTRY. IN FACT, IN MANY PHASES OF EVERYDAY
LIFE. IT ALSO INCLUDES LATE DEVELOPMENTS SUCH AS
ELECTRONIC BRAIN AND THE MUCH TALKED ABOUT TRANSISTOR.

22 MIN., SD., COLOR, 16 MM.

DEVRY TECHNICAL INSTITUTE   FREE   NAME

F0003   1954   CAB

ELECTRONICS FOR ACCOUNTING AND BUSINESS

ARTHUR ANDERSEN AND COMPANY

DEPICTS PROGRESS IN BUSINESS ACCOUNTING, SALES
FORECASTING, RECORDING, AND OTHER PROCEDURES MADE
POSSIBLE THROUGH THE INVENTION OF THE ELECTRONIC
COMPUTER. ILLUSTRATES THE PARTS OF THE MACHINE AND
THEIR FUNCTIONS, AND DISCUSSES THE NUMEROUS SAVINGS
TO BE MADE THROUGH ITS UTILIZATION.

34 MIN., SD., COLOR, 16 MM.

F0004   1954

PIERCING THE UNKNOWN

RAPHAEL WOLFF STUDIOS, INC.
PURCHASE. RAPHAEL WOLFF STUDIOS, INC. $160.00

A BRIEF LOOK AT THE HISTORICAL BACKGROUND OF DATA
PROCESSING AND SOME OF THE EARLY EQUIPMENT WHICH LED
TO TODAY'S SOLID STATE COMPUTERS. THIS FILM IS NOW
OUTDATED AND SHOULD BE USED FOR SPECIAL PURPOSES ONLY.

20 MIN., SD., COLOR, 16 MM.

IBM   FREE   NAME

F0005   1954   JSCA

UNIVAC

SEYMOUR ZWEIBEL PRODUCTIONS

A SIMPLIFIED INTRODUCTION TO THE UNIVAC ELECTRONIC
COMPUTING SYSTEM. ILLUSTRATES HOW THE SYSTEM CAN BE
APPLIED TO BUSINESS, SCIENCE, INDUSTRY, AND GOVERNMENT.

27 MIN., SD., B/W, 16 MM.

UNIVERSITY OF MICHIGAN $1.50   NAME

F0006   1955   SCA

AUTOMATIC MACHINES

CBS TV
PURCHASE. MCGRAW-HILL BOOK COMPANY $145.00

UNDER THE SUPERVISION OF THE AUTOMATIC CONTROL RESEARCH
CENTER OF MIT, THIS FILM TAKES US ON A CROSS-COUNTRY TOUR
OF LABORATORIES PIONEERING IN THE DEVELOPMENT OF NEW ROBOT
MACHINES DESIGNED TO TAKE OVER SOME OF THE DUTIES ONCE
PERFORMED EXCLUSIVELY BY THE HUMAN NERVOUS SYSTEM.
INCLUDED ARE DEMONSTRATIONS OF OUTSTANDING EXAMPLES OF
LATEST DEVELOPMENTS IN THE FIELD OF AUTOMATION.

25 MIN., SD., B/W, 16 MM.

UNIVERSITY OF CALIFORNIA	$5.00		2801
STATE UNIVERSITY OF IOWA	$4.50		U-4150
UNIVERSITY OF COLORADO	$4.25	$6.00	NAME
MICHIGAN STATE UNIVERSITY	$5.00		NAME

F0007   1955   JSCA

AUTOMATION IN TELEVISION

ATLAS FILM CORPORATION

DESCRIBES USE OF AUTOMATIC ASSEMBLY MACHINES IN PRODUCING
TELEVISION AND RADIO RECEIVERS WITH PRINTED CIRCUIT
CHASSIS.

10 MIN., SD., B/W, 16 MM.

ADMIRAL CORPORATION   FREE   NAME

F0008   1955   JSCA

AUTOMATION IS IN THE HOME

MCCALL MAGAZINE

ELIZABETH HERBERT, HOME APPLIANCE EDITOR, DESCRIBES AND
DEMONSTRATES SOME OF THE APPLIANCES THAT ARE TAKING THE
WORK OUT OF HOMEMAKING.

7 MIN., SD., B/W, 16 MM.

EDITORIAL FILMS, INC.   FREE   NAME

F0009   1955   SCA

BASE AND PLACE. (UNDERSTANDING NUMBERS SERIES)

UNIVERSITY OF MICHIGAN TELEVISION.
RELEASED BY NATIONAL EDUCATIONAL TELEVISION FILM SERVICE

PRESENTS THE CHARACTERISTICS, HISTORY, AND APPLICATIONS OF BINARY SYSTEM. EMPHASIZES THE BASIC PRINCIPLES OF BASE AND PLACE IN OUR SYSTEM OF NUMERATION. SHOWS HOW NUMBERS ARE REPRESENTED IN THE BINARY SYSTEM, ITS RELATIONSHIP TO ELECTRONIC DIGITAL COMPUTERS, AND HOW BUSINESS APPLIES THE BINARY SYSTEM. THIS IS A KINESCOPE.

30 MIN., SD., B/W, 16 MM.

UNIVERSITY OF CALIFORNIA	$5.00		5414
UNIVERSITY OF GEORGIA	$4.50		NAME
STATE UNIVERSITY OF IOWA	$4.50		U-4343
UNIVERSITY OF KENTUCKY	$5.00/WEEK		528
PENNSYLVANIA STATE UNIVERSITY	$5.75		510-3
SYRACUSE UNIVERSITY	$6.00		NAME
BRIGHAM YOUNG UNIVERSITY	$4.25	$6.00	NAME
UNIVERSITY OF COLORADO	$4.25	$6.00	NAME
UNIVERSITY OF UTAH	$4.25	$6.00	NAME
UNIVERSITY OF WYOMING	$4.25	$6.00	NAME
UNIVERSITY OF MICHIGAN	$3.00		NAME

F0010   1955   SCA

ELECTRONICS IN ACTION

RAYTHEON MANUFACTURING COMPANY
RELEASED BY ASSOCIATION FILMS 1955

TRACES HISTORY OF RAYTHEON MANUFACTURING COMPANY SINCE ITS FOUNDING IN 1922. DESCRIBES THE COMPANY'S FACILITIES AND PRODUCTS. DISCUSSES THE ELECTRONICS INDUSTRY, TOUCHING ON GUIDED MISSILES, ELECTRONIC COMPUTERS, MEDICAL DIATHERMY EQUIPMENT, VACUUM TUBES, AND SMALL TRANSISTORS.

20 MIN., SD., COLOR, 16 MM.

F0011   1956   CAB

AUTOMATION (REPORT FROM AMERICA, NO. 6)

U.S. INFORMATION AGENCY, 1956
MADE BY NATIONAL BROADCASTING COMPANY
RELEASED FOR PUBLIC EDUCATIONAL USE IN THE U.S. THROUGH U.S. OFFICE OF EDUCATION, 1958

DESCRIBES THE MEANING AND FUTURE OF AUTOMATION AS APPLIED TO LABOR, MANAGEMENT, INDUSTRY, AND POLITICS. INCLUDES INTERVIEWS WITH JOHN DIEBOLD, PETER DRUCKER, WALTER REUTHER, AND WRIGHT PATMAN. PRODUCED FOR OVERSEAS USE.

30 MIN., SD., B/W, 16 MM.

F0012   1956   JSCAB

AUTOMATION ON THE FARM

U.S. DEPARTMENT OF AGRICULTURE

DESCRIBES HOW AUTOMATION HAS COME TO THE FARM AND SHOWS THE USES OF POWER MACHINES FOR LIFTING, HAULING, ETC. FOR TV USE.

6 MIN., SD., B/W, 16 MM.

F0013   1956   CAB

ELECTRONIC COMPUTERS IMPROVE MANAGEMENT CONTROL

EDUCATIONAL FILMS UNIVERSITY OF CALIFORNIA
PURCHASE. UNIVERSITY OF CALIFORNIA $150.00

THIS FILM PRESENTS A PREDICAMENT IN A TYPICAL MANUFACTURING ORGANIZATION WHEN A LARGE CUSTOMER ORDER IS CANCELLED BECAUSE OF DELAYS IN PRODUCTION. THE HISTORY OF THE ORDER IS TRACED AND FOUND TO BE DUE TO PAPER-WORK DELAYS AND LACK OF MANAGEMENT CONTROL. A VARIETY OF BUSINESS MACHINES ARE SHOWN AND ARE APPLIED TO THE SPECIFIC PROBLEM PRESENTED IN THE FILM THUS ILLUSTRATING THE METHODS OF APPLYING ELECTRONIC DATA PROCESSING TO PROBLEMS IN MANAGEMENT CONTROL.

15 MIN., SD., COLOR, 16 MM.

UNIVERSITY OF CALIFORNIA	$10.00	3015
NEW YORK CITY COLLEGE	$5.25	NAME

F0014   1956   SCA

ELECTRONICS IN AUTOMATION

DEVRY TECHNICAL INSTITUTE

THIS FILM SHOWS MANY OPPORTUNITIES IN AUTOMATION ELECTRONICS. THE MUCH-DISCUSSED PUSH-BUTTON PLANT OF THE FUTURE IS GRAPHICALLY ILLUSTRATED, SECTION BY SECTION, WITH FULL COLOR SEQUENCES SHOWING MANY INTERESTING APPLICATIONS OF ELECTRONIC CONTROLS TO PRODUCTION PROCESSES. RECENTLY-DEVELOPED COMPUTERS AND OTHER ELECTRONIC DEVICES, VIVIDLY SHOWN, ALSO EXPLAIN THE PART AUTOMATION IS EXPECTED TO PLAY IN MODERN OFFICES.

22 MIN., SD., COLOR, 16 MM.

DEVRY TECHNICAL INSTITUTE	FREE	NAME

F0015   1956   JS

ROCKET SQUAD. (MERRIE MELODIES CARTOON)

WARNER BROTHERS CARTOONS

AN ANIMATED CARTOON ABOUT DAFFY DUCK AND PORKY PIG WHO ARE DETECTIVES OF THE TWENTY-FIFTH CENTURY INTERPLANETARY POLICE FORCE.

7 MIN., SD., COLOR, 16 MM., 35 MM.

UNIVAC DIV., SPERRY RAND CORP.	FREE	NAME

F0016   1956   SCA

THIS IS AUTOMATION

GENERAL ELECTRIC COMPANY APPARATUS SALES DIVISION
MADE BY RAPHAEL G. WOLFF STUDIOS

DEFINES THE TERM AUTOMATION AND GIVES EXAMPLES OF AUTOMATION RANGING FROM THE MANUFACTURE OF COOKIES TO CARS. SHOWS HOW IT INCREASES PRODUCTIVITY, UPGRADES WORKERS SKILLS, IMPROVES QUALITY, EXPANDS CAPACITY, AND CUTS COSTS. NUMEROUS APPLICATIONS.

30 MIN., SD., COLOR, 16 MM.

UNIVERSITY OF GEORGIA	$1.00	NAME
PENNSYLVANIA STATE UNIVERSITY	$10.00	621.8-6

F0017   1957   SCA

AUTOMATION, PART 1 OF 3 PARTS. (SEE IT NOW SERIES)

CBS TELEVISION
RELEASED BY MCGRAW-HILL BOOK COMPANY
PURCHASE. MCGRAW-HILL BOOK COMPANY (3 PARTS) $350.00

PRESENTS SEVERAL DEFINITIONS OF AUTOMATION AND TRACES THE HISTORY OF ITS DEVELOPMENT. ILLUSTRATES THE APPLICATION OF AUTOMATION AND MECHANIZATION IN THE MILLING, AIRCRAFTS, AND AUTOMOBILE INDUSTRIES, AND DISCUSSES ITS PRESENT AND FUTURE ROLES IN AIR TRAFFIC CONTROL AND IN MEDICINE. REPRESENTATIVES OF LABOR AND MANAGEMENT DISCUSS THE BENEFITS AND PROBLEMS WHICH HAVE RESULTED FROM AUTOMATION IN INDUSTRY.

36 MIN., SD., B/W, 16 MM.

UNIVERSITY OF CALIFORNIA (3 PARTS)	$17.50		4899
NEW YORK CITY COLLEGE	$4.30		NAME
PENNSYLVANIA STATE UNIVERSITY	$6.75		621.8-9
SYRACUSE UNIVERSITY (3 PARTS)	$10.50		3-3337
UNIVERSITY OF COLORADO	$4.25	$6.00	NAME
UNIVERSITY OF NEVADA	$4.25	$6.00	NAME
UNIVERSITY OF UTAH	$4.25	$6.00	NAME
UNIVERSITY OF MICHIGAN (3 PARTS)	$12.00		NAME

F0018   1957   SCA

AUTOMATION, PART 2 OF 3 PARTS. (SEE IT NOW SERIES)

CBS TELEVISION
RELEASED BY MCGRAW-HILL BOOK COMPANY

SOME INDUSTRIES HAVE BENEFITED FROM AUTOMATION IN TERMS OF A HIGHER QUALITY OF PRODUCTS, INCREASED PRODUCTION AND SERVICES, EXPANSION, A RISE IN EMPLOYMENT, AND A REVITALIZED ECONOMY IN SOME AREAS. OTHER INDUSTRIES FACE LABOR PROBLEMS CREATED BY UNEMPLOYMENT. EMPHASIZES THAT AUTOMATIC MACHINES ARE TOOLS, NOT BRAINS, AND THAT THEY RELEASE MEN FOR CREATIVE THINKING.

23 MIN., SD., B/W, 16 MM.

UNIVERSITY OF CALIFORNIA (3 PARTS)	$17.50		4899
NEW YORK CITY COLLEGE	$4.30		NAME
PENNSYLVANIA STATE UNIVERSITY	$5.25		621.8-10
SYRACUSE UNIVERSITY (3 PARTS)	$10.50		3-3337
UNIVERSITY OF COLORADO	$4.25	$6.00	NAME
UNIVERSITY OF NEVADA	$4.25	$6.00	NAME
UNIVERSITY OF UTAH	$4.25	$6.00	NAME
UNIVERSITY OF MICHIGAN (3 PARTS)	$12.00		NAME

F0019   1957   SCA

AUTOMATION, PART 3 OF 3 PARTS. (SEE IT NOW SERIES)

CBS TELEVISION
RELEASED BY MCGRAW-HILL BOOK COMPANY

DESCRIBES RUSSIA'S PROGRESS IN THE FIELD OF AUTOMATION
AND SUGGESTS THAT INDUSTRIES IN OUR COUNTRY SHOULD DEVOTE
MORE EFFORT TO THIS FIELD. ALSO DISCUSSES THE NEED FOR
A CLEARING HOUSE OF INFORMATION TO DETERMINE AUTOMATION'S
IMPACT ON THE NATIONAL ECONOMY. PRESENTS THE CHALLENGES
OF AUTOMATION TO EDUCATORS TO PROVIDE PRESENT AND FUTURE
NEEDS IN THE FIELDS OF MORE PERSONAL CREATIVE EXPRESSION
AND TECHNICAL KNOWLEDGE.

25 MIN., SD., B/W, 16 MM.

UNIVERSITY OF CALIFORNIA (3 PARTS)	$17.50		4899
NEW YORK CITY COLLEGE	$4.30		NAME
PENNSYLVANIA STATE UNIVERSITY	$5.25		621.8-11
SYRACUSE UNIVERSITY (3 PARTS)	$10.50		3-3337
UNIVERSITY OF COLORADO	$4.25	$6.00	NAME
UNIVERSITY OF NEVADA	$4.25	$6.00	NAME
UNIVERSITY OF UTAH	$4.25	$6.00	NAME
UNIVERSITY OF MICHIGAN (3 PARTS)	$12.00		NAME

F0020   1957   CA

NO MARGIN FOR ERROR

PATHE PICTURES
PURCHASE. MOVIELAB, INC. $10.00

BRIEF SUMMARY OF THE ACTIVITIES OF THE IBM MAGNETIC TAPE
TESTING CENTER AT MINNEAPOLIS WHERE MAGNETIC TAPES ARE
TESTED, MADE PERFECT, AND CAREFULLY PACKAGED UNDER HIGHEST
QUALITY CONTROL CONDITIONS TO INSURE RELIABLE COMPUTER
PERFORMANCE.

5 MIN., SD., B/W, 16 MM.

IBM	FREE	NAME

F0021   1957   JSCA

NO TIME FOR COOKIE JARS

REMINGTON RAND

BEGINNING WITH ANIMATED DESCRIPTION OF THE OLD TURNPIKE,
THE FILM EXPLAINS HOW MONEY COLLECTED FROM THE TRAVELERS
IN THE EARLY DAYS WAS SOMETIMES KEPT IN COOKIE JARS. A
COMPREHENSIVE DESCRIPTION OF THE MODERN TURNPIKE FOLLOWS,
SHOWING HOW AUTOMATION FACILITATES THE MOVEMENT OF TRAFFIC
THROUGH THE TOLL GATES AS FEES ARE COLLECTED WITH A
MINIMUM SLOWING OF TRAFFIC.

21 MIN., SD., COLOR, 16 MM.

PENNSYLVANIA STATE UNIVERSITY	$1.75	621.8-14
UNIVERSITY OF CALIFORNIA	$1.75	621.8-14
SYRACUSE UNIVERSITY	$2.50	2-3675
UNIVERSITY OF COLORADO	$1.25	NAME
UNIVERSITY OF MICHIGAN	$1.00	NAME
INDIANA UNIVERSITY	$1.15	ISC-338

F0022   1957   CA

NUMERICAL CONTROL, INDUSTRY'S ADVANCED PRODUCTION METHOD

BOEING COMPANY

FAMILIARIZES BOTH TECHNICAL AND LAY AUDIENCES WITH THE
NUMERICAL CONTROL METHOD OF AUTOMATICALLY MACHINING
COMPLEX PARTS, USING PUNCHED OR MAGNETIC TAPE FOR
ELECTRONIC DIRECTION OF ALL CUTTING OPERATIONS. OUTLINES
ENTIRELY PROCESSING OF TYPICAL PARTS, STARTING WITH
ORIGINAL ENGINEERING DRAWINGS AND EXPLAINING HOW TO
PLOT THE CUTTER PATHS, CALCULATE 3-DIMENSIONAL
DESCRIPTIONS, TRANSLATE THE DESCRIPTION INTO TAPE
COMMANDS THROUGH USE OF ELECTRONIC COMPUTERS, AND
ENDING WITH THE ACTUAL MACHINING OPERATION.

21 MIN., SD., COLOR, 16 MM.

BOEING COMPANY	FREE	NAME

F0023   1957   CAB

RAMAC

PATHE PICTURES, INC.
PURCHASE. COLOR SERVICE, INC. $75.00

A BRIEF SALES-ORIENTED TREATMENT OF BOTH THE 305 RAMAC
AND THE 650 RAMAC, EXPLAINING THE NATURE OF RANDOM ACCESS
METHOD OF ACCOUNTING AND CONTROL.

10 MIN., SD., COLOR, 16MM.

IBM	FREE	NAME

F0024   1958   CAB

AUTOMATIC INFORMATION RETRIEVAL

FDP TECHNICAL INFORMATION CENTER

DESCRIBES HOW A UNIQUE NEW TECHNICAL LITERATURE RESEARCH
SYSTEM, DEVELOPED BY THE F.P.O. TECHNICAL INFORMATION
CENTER AND EVENDALE COMPUTATIONS, CAN SEARCH THROUGH
THOUSANDS OF DOCUMENTS AND, IN A MATTER OF MINUTES, LOCATE
INFORMATION ON ANY GIVEN SUBJECT. THIS
FILM SHOWS THE RETRIEVAL SYSTEM IN ACTION, OUTLINES THE
TYPE AND DEPTH OF RESEARCH MATERIAL THE SYSTEM MAKES
READILY AVAILABLE TO A SEARCHER, AND SHOWS THE SPEED AND
SIMPLICITY WITH WHICH IT SUPPLIES THE INFORMATION SOUGHT.

13 MIN., SD., COLOR, 16MM.

GENERAL ELECTRIC COMPANY	FREE	NAME

F0025   1958   CAB

AUTOMATION AND MR. HALSTEAD

GENERAL ELECTRIC COMPANY
MADE BY RAPHAEL G. WOLFF STUDIOS

DISCUSSES THE ROLE OF ELECTRONIC EQUIPMENT AND TECHNOLOGY
IN THE DEVELOPMENT OF AUTOMAION SYSTEMS. EXPLAINS THE
NEED OF KEEPING ABREAST OF CONTINUING DEVELOPMENTS IN
ELECTRONIC TECHNOLOGY IN ORDER TO RECOGNIZE WHEN
AUTOMATION BECOMES PRACTICAL FOR A GIVEN PRODUCTION
PROBLEM. DESCRIBES THE GROWING ADVANTAGE OF AUTOMATION
AND THE NEED FOR FLEXIBILITY IN AUTOMATED PROCESSES.

28 MIN., SD., COLOR, 16 MM.

F0026   1958   CAB

THE CARDS THAT COUNT

PRODUCED BY TRANSFILM, INC.
PURCHASE. COLOR SERVICE, INC. $67.00

A DETAILED ACCOUNT OF THE METICULOUS QUALITY CONTROL
THAT ASSURES THE RELIABILITY OF THE IBM CARD. SUITABLE
FOR EDUCATION, SALES PROMOTIONAL PURPOSES. PRIMARILY
FOR AUDIENCES WITH A SPECIAL INTEREST IN PUNCHED CARDS.

15 MIN., SD., COLOR, 16 MM.

IBM	FREE	NAME

F0027   1958   SCA

COMPUTER PROGRAMMING

SYSTEM DEVELOPMENT CORPORATION

A 1958 FILM PRODUCED BY SDC AND FILMED BY UPA, ON BASIC
PROGRAMMING. WHAT IT IS ABOUT, WHAT THE PROGRAMMER DOES,
HOW AND WHY HE DOES IT. A GOOD FILM TO SHOW TO LOGICALLY-
MINDED PROSPECTIVE PROGRAMMERS OR THOSE INTERESTED IN
KNOWING WHAT A PROGRAMMER DOES. IT IS SOMEWHAT DATED AS
TO ACTUAL TECHNIQUES AND EXTREMELY BASIC IN CERTAIN AREAS.

26 MIN., SD., B/W, 16 MM.

SYSTEM DEVELOPMENT CORPORATION	FREE	XF-8

F0028   1958   SCA

HAVE I TOLD YOU LATELY I LOVE YOU

DEPT. OF CINEMA, UNIVERSITY OF SOUTHERN CALIFORNIA

A SYMBOLIC RECORD OF ONE DAY IN THE LIFE OF THE MEMBERS
OF AN UPPER-MIDDLE CLASS AMERICAN FAMILY SHOWING THEIR

DEPENDENCE ON MACHINES AND THE EFFECT OF AUTOMATION ON
THEIR RELATIONSHIPS WITH EACH OTHER. A DISTURBING FILM
PRESENTATION OF THE OBVERSE SIDE OF AUTOMATION,
FRAGMENTING AND MECHANOID OVERTONES THAT COULD HELP TAKE
OVER THE ESSENTIALS.

17 MIN., SD., B/W, 16 MM.

F0029   1958   JSCA

THE INFORMATION MACHINE

CHARLES EAMES AND RAY EAMES
MADE AND RELEASED BY IBM CORP.
PURCHASE. CHARLES EAMES PRODUCTION $60.00

A SOPHISTICATED, AMUSING ACCOUNT OF THE DEVELOPMENT OF
THE ELECTRONIC COMPUTER BEGINNING WITH PRIMITIVE MAN AND
ENDING WITH THE ADVENT OF MACHINE SIMULATION. COLORFUL
AND IMAGINATIVE, THIS FILM IS AN EFFECTIVE COMMUNICATIONS
DEVICE FOR EXPLAINING THE NATURE OF DATA PROCESSING.

10 MIN., SD., COLOR, 16MM., 35 MM.

| IBM | FREE | NAME |

F0030   1958   CAB

INFORMATION MACHINE

EAMES PRODUCTIONS

ANIMATED PRESENTATION TO INFORM BUSINESSMEN AS TO WHAT
COMPUTERS CAN AND CANNOT DO, FOR DISCUSSION OF AUTOMATION,
FOR STUDY OF PHOTOGRAPHIC TECHNIQUES.

11 MIN., SD., COLOR, 16 MM.

| PENNSYLVANIA STATE UNIVERSITY | $3.75 | 651.26-1 |
| SYSTEM DEVELOPMENT CORPORATION | FREE | XF-13 |

F0031   1958   CA

INTRODUCTION TO AUTOMATIC DATA PROCESSING

U.S. DEPT. OF THE ARMY

EXPLAINS UNDERLYING CONCEPT, CAPABILITIES, OPERATION
AND APPLICATION AS A NEW MANAGEMENT TOOL,SYSTEMS IN USE
IN GOVERNMENT INSTALLATIONS, PRESENT AND POSSIBLE FUTURE
USES OF ADPS IN ARMY RELATIVE TO ADMINISTRATIVE AND
TACTICAL ASPECTS.

31 MIN., SD., B/W, 16 MM.

| U.S. ARMY | FREE | TF 11-2552 |

F0032   1958   CAB

THE NATURE OF WORK - THE SKILLED WORKER (WORLD IN ACTION)

NATIONAL FILM BOARD OF CANADA
RELEASED IN U.S. BY MCGRAW-HILL BOOK COMPANY
PURCHASE. MCGRAW-HILL BOOK COMPANY $135.00

CONSIDERS THE DISPLACEMENT OF SKILLED WORKERS BY THE
MACHINE, TELLING THE STORY OF AN IMMIGRANT FROM THE
UKRAINE WHO, AFTER COMING TO CANADA, LEARNS THE MACHINIST'S
TRADE AND BRINGS TO HIS JOB PRIDE IN CRAFTSMANSHIP, AND
WHOSE WORLD CRUMBLES WHEN THE COMPANY BRINGS IN AUTOMATIC
EQUIPMENT TO DO THE WORK WHICH FOR YEARS HAS BEEN DONE
BY MEN.

30 MIN., SD., B/W, 16MM.

F0033   1958   CAB

THE NEW GIANT

HUGHES AIRCRAFT COMPANY

A LOOK INTO THE UNBELIEVABLY COMPLEX WORLD OF MILITARY
ELECTRONICS. THIS FILM, A BUSINESS/INDUSTRY AWARD WINNER
AT THE 1958 COLUMBUS FILM FESTIVAL, EXAMINES THE
TREMENDOUS GROWTH OF A NEW INDUSTRY AND EMPHASIZES THE
VITAL ROLE PLAYED BY HIGHLY SKILLED HUMAN BEINGS IN THE
CREATION OF AIRBORNE AUTOMATION.

15 MIN., SD., COLOR, 16 MM.

| HUGHES AIRCRAFT COMPANY | FREE | NAME |

F0034   1958   CAB

NEW HORIZONS IN MATERIALS HANDLING

BARRETT-CRAVENS COMPANY
MADE BY REID H. RAY INDUSTRY

THIS FILM SURVEYS THE ENGINEERING AND MANUFACTURING OF
MATERIALS HANDLING SYSTEMS BY BARRETT-CRAVENS COMPANY
WITH EMPHASIS ON AUTOMATED MACHINES. DISCUSSES THE
APPLICATION OF THE AUTOMATED, GUID-O-MATIC TRACTOR TO
TRAFFIC AND WORK FLOW CONDITIONS IN FACTORIES AND
WAREHOUSES.

20 MIN., SD., COLOR, 16 MM.

| NEW YORK CITY COLLEGE | $5.00 | NAME |

F0035   1958   SCA

QUICKER THAN YOU THINK. (THE DIGITAL COMPUTER)

WESTINGHOUSE BROADCASTING COMPANY
PURCHASE. NDEA

DISCUSSES THE EVOLUTION OF PRIMITIVE COUNTING SYSTEMS
INTO THE MODERN ELECTRONIC CALCULATOR BASED ON THE BINARY
SYSTEM. EXPLAINS THAT MAN MUST PLAN THE WORK EVEN THOUGH
THE CALCULATOR WORKS AT THE SPEED OF LIGHT. FEATURES BILL
BAIRD AND HIS MARIONETTES.

30 MIN., SD., B/W, 16 MM.

| ASSOCIATION FILMS, INC. | $7.50 | EW-402 |

F0036   1958   SCA

THE SEARCH AT SAN JOSE

ON FILMS, INC.
PURCHASE. ON FILMS, INC. $60.00

THE STORY, TOLD IN STYLIZED FASHION, OF HOW RAMAC WAS
DEVELOPED. AN INSIDE LOOK INTO THE INTER-RELATIONSHIPS
OF MARKET RESEARCH, ENGINEERING, PRODUCT DEVELOPMENT,
SALES, PRODUCTION, AS RAMAC EVOLVED FROM AN IDEA INTO
PRODUCTION LINE COMPUTERS STREAMING OUT OF A MODERN PLANT.

12 MIN., SD., COLOR, B/W, 16 MM.

| IBM | FREE | NAME |

F0037   1958   CAB

SERVO SYSTEMS AND DATA TRANSMISSION

U.S. NAVY

THIS FILM PRESENTS A STUDY OF AUTOMATIC SERVO AND DATA
TRANSMISSION SYSTEMS, DEFINING THEIR INTER-RELATIONSHIP
AND APPLICATION IN TRACKING ENEMY TARGET INFORMATION.

33 MIN., SD., B/W, 16 MM.

| U.S. NAVY | FREE | NAME |

F0038   1959   CA

ASTIA (ARMED SERVICES TECHNICAL INFORMATION AGENCY)

U.S. DEPT. OF AIR FORCE

FILM OUTLINES SCOPE AND MISSION OF THE ARMED SERVICES
TECHNICAL INFORMATION AGENCY AND POINTS OUT ITS IMPORTANCE
TO OUR RESEARCH AND DEVELOPMENT PROGRAM. PROCEDURES FOR
UTILIZING ASTIA SERVICES ARE ALSO COVERED.

15 MIN., SD., COLOR, 16 MM.

| U.S.A.F FILM LIBRARY CENTER | FREE | NAME |

F0039   1959   CAB

AUTOMATION, WHAT IS IT. (INDUSTRY ON PARADE, NO. 462)

NATIONAL ASSOCIATION OF MANUFACTURES

EXPLAINS THAT AUTOMATION IS THE LATEST EXTENTION OF
INDUSTRY'S CONTINUING DEVELOPMENT OF IMPROVED MANUFACTURING
METHODS. DESCRIBES HOW AUTOMATION IS APPLIED IN A SAWMILL,
IN THE HANDLING OF COMMERCIAL MAIL, IN OIL REFINING, IN
THE MANUFACTURE OF LACE, IN THE TELEPHONE INDUSTRY, AND
IN FARMING.

14 MIN., SD., B/W, 16 MM.

F0040   1959   CAB

DATA PROCESSING FOR HOSPITALS

DPD PROMOTIONAL SERVICES, WHITE PLAINS, NEW YORK
PURCHASE. PRECISION FILM LABORATORIES, INC. $100.00

STORY OF A RAMAC 305 USED IN HOSPITAL ACCOUNTING.
PHOTOGRAPHY WAS SHOT LIVE AT THE NEW YORK COLISEUM
DURING THE MACHINE DEMONSTRATION AT AN AMERICAN HOSPITAL
ASSOCIATION CONVENTION.

16 MIN., SD., COLOR, 16 MM.

IBM	FREE	NAME

F0041   1959   JS

DONALD IN MATHMAGIC LAND

WALT DISNEY PRODUCTIONS, INC.

PROOF THAT MATH NEED NOT NECESSARILY BE DULL AND BORING.
DONALD DUCK LEARNS THE IMPORTANCE OF MATHEMATICS FROM
EARLY GREEKS WHO DISCOVERED SOME OF ITS BASIC PRINCIPLES.
LATER SEQUENCES SHOW HOW THESE PRINCIPLES ARE RELATED TO
MUSIC, ART, ARCHITECTURE, MECHANICS, SPORTS, AND OTHER
PHASES OF OUR DAILY LIVES. BOTH ANIMATION AND LIVE ACTION
PHOTOGRAPHY ARE USED.

26 MIN., SD., COLOR, 16 MM.

UNIVERSITY OF CALIFORNIA	$12.50		3226
UNIVERSITY OF KENTUCKY	$5.00		543
SYRACUSE UNIVERSITY	$8.75		3-3474
BRIGHAM YOUNG UNIVERSITY	$5.75	$8.50	NAME
UNIVERSITY OF UTAH	$5.75	$8.50	NAME
MICHIGAN STATE UNIVERSITY	$10.00		NAME
UNIVERSITY OF MICHIGAN	$10.00		NAME
ASSOCIATION FILMS, INC.	$12.00		WX-532

F0042   1959   JSCA

EGGS BY AUTOMATION

HOTCHKISS COLORFILM PRODUCTIONS
PURCHASE. HOTCHKISS COLORFILM PROD. $85.00 CL,$50.00 B/W

HOW ELECTRO-MECHANICAL PRINCIPLES CAN LIGHTEN HUMAN
LABOR, REDUCE FOOD COSTS, SPEED MARKETING OF FARM PRODUCTS.
FOLLOWS EGGS FROM FARM TO BREAKFAST TABLE THROUGH
INCREDIBLE MECHANICAL STEPS THAT CLEARLY REVEAL MEANING
OF AUTOMATION.

10 MIN., SD., COLOR, B/W, 16 MM.

UNIVERSITY OF MICHIGAN	$4.00	NAME

F0043   1959   SCA

HUGHES ELECTRONIC NEWS

HUGHES AIRCRAFT COMPANY

A REGULARLY UP-DATED NEWSREEL REPORT OF INTERESTING
DEVELOPMENT ACTIVITIES AT HUGHES. TYPICAL SUBJECTS
INCLUDE ELECTRON TUBE PRODUCTION, THE GAR-3 SUPER FALCON,
TRANSISTOR MANUFACTURING, THE FIRST FULLY AUTOMATED
PRODUCTION LINE, NEW DIODE PRODUCTION FACILITIES AND
TECHNIQUE, THE RUBY LASER, RAMAC, MISSILE MONITOR, ION
ENGINE, FREEWAYS AND ELECTRONICS, ELECTROCULAR, MOBOT,
FRESCAN, SYNCOM, SURVEYOR, AND BIO-INSTRUMENTATION KIT.

15 MIN., SD., COLOR, 16 MM.

HUGHES AIRCRAFT CO.	FREE	NAME

F0044   1959   SCA

INTERCEPT

STAN RUSSELL PRODUCTIONS
PURCHASE. DEPARTMENT 808, IBM KINGSTON $50.00

HOW THE SAGE/BOMARC AIR DEFENSE SYSTEM OPERATES TO SECURE
OUR BORDERS FROM ENEMY AIR ATTACK. A GIANT IBM COMPUTER
IN A SAGE INSTALLATION TRACKS THE TARGET AUTOMATICALLY.
IT FIRES THE MISSILE FROM A LAUNCHING POINT HUNDREDS OF
MILES AWAY, AND GUIDES THE MISSILE IN FLIGHT TO ITS TARGET.

10 MIN., SD., COLOR, 16 MM.

IBM	FREE	NAME

F0045   1959   CA

TRANSISTOR-SWITCHING

U.S. NAVY DEPT.

THIS FILM SHOWS EXAMPLES OF SWITCHING CIRCUITS IN
TRANSISTORIZED COMPUTERS; EXPLAINING BRIEFLY THE CONCEPT
OF DIGITAL COMPUTATION AND HOW TRANSISTORS ARE USED.
THE FILM INCLUDES A MORE DETAILED EXPLANATION OF HOW A
SIMPLE TRANSLATOR SWITCH WORKS, MINORITY CARRIER STORAGE
IN THE BASE, AND HOW DELAYING EFFECTS OF THIS STORAGE
ARE OVERCOME.

14 MIN., SD., B/W, 16 MM.

U.S. NAVY	FREE	NAME

F0046   1959   JSCA

X-15..MAN INTO SPACE

IBM CORPORATION
MADE BY SPOTLIGHT NEWS
PURCHASE. FILM AND TV NEWS ACTIVITIES DEPT., CHQ $25.00

THE STORY OF THE COMBINED EFFORT OF THE U.S. AIR FORCE,
NASA, AND THE NORTH AMERICAN AVIATION COMPANY TO FLY A
MAN TO THE EDGE OF OUTER SPACE. FILMED IN STRIKING COLOR,
THE PICTURE INCLUDES COVERAGE OF THE X-15 ROCKET PLANE
BEING CARRIED ALOFT BY A GIANT B-52 JET BOMBER, AND ITS
ACTUAL DROP. GRAPHIC ANIMATION THEN TAKES THE VIEWER
ALONG AS THE X-15 CLIMBS TO A HEIGHT OF MORE THAN 100
MILES ABOVE THE EARTH. ALSO GRAPHICALLY DESCRIBES IBM'S
PARTICIPATION IN THIS PROJECT THROUGH COMPUTERS WHICH
ANALYZE THE X-15 PERFORMANCE IN THIS QUEST FOR INFORMATION
WHICH WILL HELP TO LEAD MAN TO THE PLANETS.

8 MIN., SD., COLOR, 16 MM. 35 MM.

IBM	FREE	NAME

F0047   1960   JSCA

AUTOMATION IN AIR TRAFFIC CONTROL

UNIVAC, SPERRY RAND CORP.

SHOWS THE DETAILED DATA-PROCESSING PROCEDURES INVOLVED
IN A TYPICAL FLIGHT FROM BOSTON TO WASHINGTON, FOLLOWING
THE FLIGHT FROM THE FILING OF THE FLIGHT PLAN TO ARRIVAL
AT THE DESTINATION. EXAMPLES ARE SHOWN TO ILLUSTRATE HOW
THE UNIVAC FILE-COMPUTER HANDLES EACH PHASE OF THE FLIGHT,
COMPENSATING FOR, AND CORRECTING SUCH VARIABLES AS LATE
TAKE-OFF AND CONFLICTING FLIGHT PLANS.

11 MIN., SD., COLOR, 16 MM.

UNIVERSITY OF CALIFORNIA	$2.00	5603
PENNSYLVANIA STATE UNIVERSITY	$1.50	621.8-12
SYRACUSE UNIVERSITY	$2.50	1-3677
UNIVERSITY OF COLORADO	$1.25	NAME
UNIVERSITY OF MICHIGAN	$1.00	NAME
UNIVAC DIV., SPERRY RAND CORP.	FREE	NAME
INDIANA UNIVERSITY	$1.15	ASC-54

F0048   1960   JSCA

CENSUS SIXTY

UNIVAC, SPERRY RAND CORP

EXPLAINS WHY A CENSUS IS NEEDED, HOW THE INFORMATION IS
GATHERED, AND THE PART PLAYED BY ELECTRONIC COMPUTERS IN
ANALYZING AND SUMMARIZING THE RESULTS.

15 MIN., SD., B/W, 16MM.

UNIVERSITY OF CALIFORNIA	$2.00	5604
PENNSYLVANIA STATE UNIVERSITY	$1.75	621.8-13
UNIVERSITY OF COLORADO	$1.25	NAME
UNIVERSITY OF MICHIGAN	$1.00	NAME
UNIVAC DIV., SPERRY RAND CORP.	FREE	NAME
INDIANA UNIVERSITY	$1.15	IS-339

F0049   1960   JSCA

THE COMPUTER IN THE CLASSROOM

RAND CORPORATION

DEPICTS BY CANDID PHOTOGRAPHY A GROUP OF GIFTED NINTH
AND TENTH GRADERS AS THEY RESPOND TO A SUMMER COURSE
DEVOTED TO PRACTICE AT A LGP-30 COMPUTER, TO PROGRAMMING.

FLOWCHARTING, TESTING, AND EXPLANATIONS TO COMPUTER
CIRCUITRY AND COMPUTER CHESS.

13 MIN., SD., B/W, 16 MM.

RAND CORPORATION	FREE	NAME

F0050   .1960   CA

INTRODUCTION TO FEEDBACK

CHARLES EAMES AND RAY EAMES
PURCHASE. CHARLES EAMES PRODUCTIONS $60.00

THE CYCLE OF MEASURING, EVALUATING, AND CORRECTING IS
CALLED FEEDBACK. IT HAS BECOME A SCIENCE AND AN ART.
THIS FILM IS A SIMPLE PRESENTATION OF THE FEEDBACK IDEA,
ITS GROWING IMPORTANCE IN OUR CULTURE AND SOME EXAMPLES
OF TOOLS TO FACILITATE ITS USE, SUCH AS ELECTRONIC DATA
PROCESSING.

12 MIN., SD., COLOR, 16 MM.

IBM	FREE	NAME

F0051   1960   CA

LEARNING AND BEHAVIOR. (THE TEACHING MACHINE)

CBS NEWS
PURCHASE. CAROUSEL FILMS, INC. $135.00

AN ENLIGHTENING FILM ON HOW SCIENCE CAN ACTUALLY MEASURE
THE LEARNING PROCESS. FILMED AT HARVARD UNIVERSITY'S
PSYCHOLOGY LABORATORY, WE SEE HOW DRS. B.F. SKINNER AND
R.J. HERRNSTEIN MEASURE LEARNING AND CONDITIONING IN THE
LABORATORY, THEREBY UNCOVERING IMPORTANT KNOWLEDGE ABOUT
ONE OF THE MOST FUNDAMENTAL PROCESSES OF BEHAVIOR.

26 MIN., SD., B/W, 16 MM.

HAMILTON FILM SERVICE	$10.00	NAME
CAROUSEL FILMS, INC.	$15.00	NAME

F0052   1960   SCA

MANPOWER BANK OF THE AIR FORCE

U.S. DEPT. OF AIR FORCE

TWO RESERVISTS VISIT THE AIR RESERVE RECORDS CENTER AT
DENVER, COLORADO, WHERE MORE THAN ONE-HALF MILLION RECORDS
ARE MAINTAINED VIA AUTOMATION AND A SPECIAL TERMINAL DIGIT
FILING SYSTEM. HERE, THEY SEE HOW THE DATA OF EACH
RESERVIST IS PROCESSED AND ENTERED IN HIS SERVICE RECORD.
THEY ALSO LEARN OF THE IMPORTANCE OF KEEPING THE CENTER
INFORMED OF NEW SKILLS, EDUCATION, AND EXPERIENCE GAINED,
AND OF THEIR PARTICIPATION IN LOCAL RETIREMENT, CAREER
FIELD, OPPORTUNITIES FOR PROMOTION, ETC.

18 MIN., SD., B/W, 16 MM.

U.S.A.F. FILM LIBRARY CENTER	FREE	SFP 672

F0053   1960   CA

MEMORY DEVICES

BELL TELEPHONE LABORATORIES
RELEASED BY BELL TELEPHONE SYSTEM

BASIC CONCEPTS OF INFORMATION STORAGE DEVICES AND
EXAMPLES OF MECHANICAL, ELECTROMECHANICAL, MAGNETIC,
ELECTROSTATIC AND PHOTOGRAPHIC MEMORIES ARE DESCRIBED.
THIS TECHNICAL FILM SHOWS HOW BINARY INFORMATION IS
STORED IN COMPUTERS.

28 MIN., SD., COLOR, 16 MM.

WESTERN ELECTRIC	FREE	NAME

F0054   1960   CAB

MEMORY INCORPORATED

UNION CARBIDE NUCLEAR COMPANY

THIS FILM SHOWS HOW THE USE OF COMPUTERS HAS INCREASED
THE EFFICIENCY OF THE PLANT'S STOCK AND INVENTORY CONTROL
ACTIVITIES. THE FILM IS NOTABLE FOR ITS DETAILED
ANALYSIS OF HOW THE PRESENT SYSTEM WAS PERFECTED AND
THE EASE WITH WHICH IT IS OPERATED. IT TRACES THE
INVENTORY STORY FROM THE TIME AN EMPLOYEE TAKES AN ITEM

OUT OF STOCK TO WHEN THE PURCHASING AGENT ARRANGES FOR
A REORDER

12 MIN., SD., COLOR, 16 MM.

UNION CARBIDE NUCLEAR CO.	FREE	NAME

F0055   1960   SCA

ON GUARD-ON TARGET

HUGHES AIRCRAFT COMPANY

EVEN AFTER INTERCONTINENTAL BALLISTIC MISSILES ARE
AVAILABLE IN LARGE QUANTITIES, MANNED BOMBERS WITH THEIR
PIN-POINT ACCURACY WILL CONTINUE TO BE A MAJOR THREAT
TO THE UNITED STATES. THIS FILM DESCRIBES NORAD (NORTH
AMERICAN AIR DEFENSE) THE INVISIBLE SHIELD, COMPRISED
OF DISTANT EARLY WARNING LINES OF DETECTION, PICKET
SHIPS, PICKET PLANES, TEXAS TOWERS AND ALWAYS READY
INTERCEPTORS WHICH PROTECT US, DAY AND NIGHT, AGAINST
ANY SURPRISE ATTACK.

10 MIN., SD., COLOR, 16 MM.

HUGHES AIRCRAFT COMPANY	FREE	NAME

F0056   1960   CA

PUSH-BUTTONS AND PEOPLE

UNITED AUTOMOBILE WORKERS OF AMERICA
PURCHASE. CONTEMPORARY FILMS, INC. $100.00

PRESENTS THE ROLE THAT AUTOMATION IS ASSUMING AND WILL
PLAY IN OUR SOCIETY. WALTER REUTHER, PRESIDENT OF THE
U.A.W., STATES LABOR'S POSITION ON THE AUTOMATION ISSUE
AND THE BENEFITS AND DISADVANTAGES OF AUTOMATION.

22 MIN., SD., B/W, 16 MM.

NEW YORK CITY COLLEGE	$4.75	NAME
CONTEMPORARY FILMS, INC.	$7.00	NAME

F0057   1960   JSC

SCIENCE PROJECT

VISUAL EDUCATION FILMS
PURCHASE. INTERNATIONAL FILM BUREAU, INC. $150.00

THE PURPOSE OF THIS FILM IS TO ACTIVATE STUDENT INTEREST
IN SCIENTIFIC INVESTIGATION BY THE PROJECT METHOD. THE
FILM RECORDS A BOY'S ADVENTURE PREPARING HIS FIRST SCIENCE
PROJECT, HIS SEARCH FOR A PROJECT IDEA, RESEARCH, PLANNING
AND BUILDING AND THE EXHIBITION OF THE PROJECT (A SIMPLE
COMPUTER) AT A SCIENCE FAIR.

14 MIN., SD., COLOR, 16MM.

UNIVERSITY OF CALIFORNIA	$6.00	5657
SYRACUSE UNIVERSITY	$5.75	2-4401
UNIVERSITY OF MICHIGAN	$4.50	NAME
INTERNATIONAL FILM BUREAU, INC.	$6.00	NAME

F0058   1960   CA

TEACHING MACHINES AND PROGRAMMED LEARNING

U.S. OFFICE OF EDUCATION
MADE BY NATIONAL EDUCATION ASSOCIATION
NORWOOD FILMS

TRACES THE MOVEMENT FROM THE EARLY DEVELOPMENT OF
TEACHING MACHINES TO THE PRESENT DAY CONCEPT OF PROGRAMMED
MATERIALS AND AUTO-INSTRUCTIONAL LEARNING BY NOTABLE
AUTHORITIES SUCH AS SKINNER, GLASSER AND OTHERS. IN A
SENSE IT IS A BASIC PRIMER FOR THIS NEW FIELD ON FILM
GIVING MANY ILLUSTRATIONS OF THE VARIOUS TYPES OF SELF-
INSTRUCTIONAL MEDIA.

29 MIN., SD., B/W, 16MM.

UNIVERSITY OF GEORGIA	$2.00		NAME
SYRACUSE UNIVERSITY	$6.00		3-3775
COLORADO STATE COLLEGE	$4.25	$6.00	NAME
UNIVERSITY OF UTAH	$4.25	$6.00	NAME
UNIVERSITY OF COLORADO	$4.25	$6.00	NAME
MICHIGAN STATE UNIVERSITY	$5.50		NAME
UNIVERSITY OF MICHIGAN	$5.50		NAME

F0059   1960   JSCA

THE THINKING MACHINE

CBS NEWS
PURCHASE. ASSOCIATION FILMS, INC.

A FILM REPORT ON THE ONLY TWO KNOWN OBJECTS IN THE
UNIVERSE THAT SEEM CAPABLE OF REASONING, THE HUMAN
BRAIN AND THE ELECTRONIC DIGITAL COMPUTER. WE SEE
A TELEVISION PLAY WRITTEN BY A COMPUTER, WATCH A
COMPUTER THAT SEEMS TO LEARN AS A CHILD LEARNS, AND
SEE A COMPUTER PLAYING CHECKERS (AND WINNING). WE
LEARN WHY SOME AUTHORITIES BELIEVE THAT THE ELECTRONIC
COMPUTER MAY CHANGE THE WORLD.

54 MIN., SD., B/W, 16 MM.

SYRACUSE UNIVERSITY	$11.00	3-3734
UNIVERSITY OF MICHIGAN	$7.50	NAME
HAMILTON FILM SERVICE	$15.00	NAME
CAROUSEL FILMS, INC.	$25.00	NAME
INDIANA UNIVERSITY	$9.15	ES-599

F0060   1960   JSCA

THINKING MACHINES. (HORIZONS OF SCIENCE SERIES)

EDUCATIONAL TESTING SERVICE
PURCHASE. EDUCATIONAL TESTING SERVICE $210.00

WITH CLAUDE SHANNON OF MIT, ALEX BERNSTEIN OF IBM, AND
LEON HARMON OF BELL LABORATORIES, THIS FILM SHOWS
APPROACHES AND EXPERIMENTS IN MACHINE INTELLIGENCE. A
MECHANICAL MOUSE THAT LEARNS BY TRIAL AND ERROR, A CHESS
GAME AGAINST A GIANT COMPUTER, AND A MACHINE THAT
RECOGNIZES VISUAL PATTERNS ARE HIGHLIGHTS. WITH
DISCUSSION AND STUDY GUIDE.

19 MIN., SD., COLOR, 16 MM.

UNIVERSITY OF CALIFORNIA	$5.00	5595
UNIVERSITY OF GEORGIA	$5.00	NAME
STATE UNIVERSTIY OF IOWA	$.75	I-5369
UNIVERSITY OF KETNUCKY	$1.00	6189
SYRACUSE UNIVERSITY	$2.50	2-3667
BRIGHAM YOUNG UNIVERSITY	$1.25	NAME
UNIVERSTIY OF COLORADO	$1.25	NAME
UNIVERSITY OF NEVADA	$1.25	NAME
UNIVERSITY OF UTAH	$1.25	NAME
UNIVERSITY OF WYOMING	$1.25	NAME
MICHIGAN STATE UNIVERSITY	$7.00	NAME
UNIVERSITY OF MICHIGAN	$7.00	NAME
INDIANA UNIVERSITY	$1.15	$ISC-316

F0061   1960   SCA

WESTWARD THE FLAME

JOHN SUTHERLAND PRODUCTIONS, INC.
PURCHASE. JOHN SUTHERLAND PRODUCTIONS, INC.

NARRATED BY LOWELL THOMAS, THIS FILM OUTLINES THE PLANS
MADE FOR THE 1960 WINTER OLYMPIC GAMES AT SQUAW VALLEY,
CALIFORNIA IN 1960. IT INCLUDES SCENES OF THE IBM
OLYMPIC DATA PROCESSING CENTER...AND SOME OF THE
OUTSTANDING SKI AND SKATING EVENTS AT THE WINTER OLYMPICS
AT OSLO, NORWAY,IN 1952 AND CORTINA, ITALY,IN 1956.

SD., COLOR, 16 MM.

IBM	FREE	NAME

F0062   1960   SCA

WHAT DO YOU WANT

UNIVAC

TRACES THE DEVELOPMENT OF ELECTRONIC COMPUTERS FROM ENIAC
TO UNIVAC III. EMPHASIZES HOW UNIVAC, BACKED BY THE
RESOURCES OF SPERRY RAND, PIONEERED AND WILL CONTINUE TO
BE A LEADER IN THE DEVELOPMENT AND PRODUCTION OF COMPUTING
SYSTEMS. J.P. ECKERT, CO-INVENTOR OF THE FIRST DIGITAL
COMPUTER, GIVES A GLIMPSE AT THE COMPUTERS OF THE FUTURE,
EXPLORING SUCH AREAS AS SPEED, STORAGE AND APPLICATION.

20 MIN., SD., COLOR, 16MM.

UNIVAC DIV, SPERRY RAND CORP.	FREE	NAME

F0063   1961   SCA

AEROSPACE COMMUNICATIONS - THE REINS OF COMMAND

U.S. DEPT. OF AIR FORCE

BRIG. GENERAL JAMES STEWART, USAFR, TELLS ABOUT THE USAF'S
VAST COMMUNICATIONS NETWORK UPON WHICH HINGE EFFECTIVE
COMMAND AND CONTROL OF THE WORLDWIDE STRIKE FORCES. HE
EXPLAINS THE OPERATION OF THE NETWORK THAT ALERTS THE
FREE WORLD TO APPROACHING HOSTILE AIRCRAFT AND MISSILE
ATTACK.

26 MIN., SD., COLOR, 16 MM.

U.S.A.F. FILM LIBRARY CENTER	FREE	SFP 1031
LOCKHEED MISSILE AND SPACE CO.	FREE	NAME

F0064   1961   C B

AUTOMATIC TELEPHONE CENTRAL OFFICES. PART 1 OF 2

U.S. DEPT. OF ARMY

THIS FILM DESCRIBES THE FEATURES, CAPABILITIES, OPERATION,
AND USE OF STOWAGER TYPE SWITCHING SYSTEMS IN MILITARY DIAL
TELEPHONE SERVICE.

26 MIN., SD., B/W, 16 MM.

U.S. ARMY	FREE	TF 11-3089

F0065   1961   C B

AUTOMATIC TELEPHONE CENTRAL OFFICES. PART 2 OF 2

U.S. DEPT. OF ARMY

THIS FILM DEPICTS THE ORGANIZATION AND OPERATION OF XY
SWITCHING SYSTEMS USED IN AUTOMATIC TELEPHONE (DIAL)
CENTRAL OFFICES. DESCRIBES THE ADVANTAGES OF XY SWITCHING
EQUIPMENT IN TERMS OF ECONOMY AND SMALL SPACE REQUIREMENTS.

30 MIN., SD., B/W, 16 MM.

U.S. ARMY	FREE	TF 11-3090

F0066   1961   SCA

AUTOPROMPT

IBM
PURCHASE. GOTHAM FILM SERVICE $5.00

THIS TWO-MINUTE MOVIE IS A DEMONSTRATION OF AUTOPROMPT
IN ACTION. IT DESCRIBES THE PROCESSING FLOW WITH
AUTOPROMPT FROM BLUEPRINT TO FINISHED PRODUCTION OF A
HELICOPTER GEARBOX COVER.

2 MIN., SD., B/W, 16 MM.

IBM	FREE	NAME

F0067   1961   CAB

BREAKTHROUGH (PERT)

SPECIAL PROJECTS OFFICE, U.S. NAVY
MADE AND RELEASED BY MERIT FILM PRODUCTIONS
PURCHASE. MERIT PRODUCTION OF CALIFORNIA $168.00

PROGRAM EVALUATION AND REVIEW TECHNIQUE IS A U.S. NAVY
METHOD FOR EVALUATING PROGRESS TO IMPROVE THE PLANNING
OF A MAJOR RESEARCH AND DEVELOPMENT PROGRAM. THIS MOVIE
DESCRIBES HOW THE U.S. NAVY USES PERT IN THE FLEET
BALLISTICS MISSILE PROGRAM. IT CAN BE USED AS A PART
OF A LEAST COST ESTIMATING AND SCHEDULING (LESS)
PRESENTATION. SUITABLE FOR BOTH IBM AND CUSTOMER VIEWING.

35 MIN., SD., COLOR, 16MM.

IBM	FREE	NAME

F0068   1961   JSCA

CITY AT NIGHT...MATHEMATICA EXHIBIT

KTLA, LOS ANGELES
PURCHASE. FILM AND TV NEWS ACTIVITIES DEPT., CHQ $50.00

ORIGINALLY TELECAST BY TV STATION KTLA IN LOS ANGELES.
FEATURES A TOUR THROUGH THE IBM-SPONSORED MATHEMATICS
EXHIBIT AT THE CALIFORNIA MUSEUM OF SCIENCE AND INDUSTRY

IN LOS ANGELES. HOST BILL STOUT INTERVIEWS CAL TECH
PHYSICIST-MATHEMATICIAN DR. ALBERT HIBBS, DESIGNER
CHARLES EAMES AND IBM MATHEMATICAIN DR. E.C. SMITH.
KINESCOPE.

45 MIN., SD., B/W, 16 MM.

IBM	FREE	NAME

F0069   1961   C B

COSTS THAT MAKE SENSE

DPD PROMOTION SERVICE
PURCHASE. PRECISION FILM LABORATORIES, INC $60.00

DEMONSTRATION OF THE IBM 1401 DATA PROCESSING SYSTEM
AT THE AMERICAN TRUCKING ASSOCIATION CONFERENCE IN
SAN FRANCISCO. IT DESCRIBES THIS MOTOR FREIGHT
APPLICATION IN DETAIL. BEST SUITED FOR THOSE WITH A
PARTICULAR INTEREST IN AND KNOWLEDGE OF THE MOTOR FREIGHT
INDUSTRY.

15 MIN., SD., COLOR, 16 MM.

IBM	FREE	NAME

F0070   1961   CA

DIGITAL COMPUTER PROGRAMMING

PURDUE UNIVERSITY

A FILMED LECTURE ON HOW TO PROGRAM INFORMATION FOR USE
IN A COMPUTER. DISCUSSED IS THE LANGUAGE OF THE COMPUTER
AND THE DETAILED WAY IN WHICH THE COMPUTER USES THE
INFORMATION THAT IS FED INTO IT.

51 MIN., SD., B/W, 16 MM.

PURDUE UNIVERSITY	$6.00	NAME

F0071   1961   C B

DISKS THAT ARE A CYLINDER

DPD PROMOTIONAL SERVICES
PURCHASE. PRECISION FILM LABORATORIES $30.00

EXPLAINS THE CONCEPT OF IBM 1301 DISK STORAGE UNIT.
BEST SUITED FOR AUDIENCES WITH SOME KNOWLEDGE OF COMPUTER
MEMORY STORAGE CONCEPTS.

10 MIN., SD., COLOR, 16MM.

IBM	FREE	NAME

F0072   1961   JSCA

ELECTRONIC COMPUTERS AND APPLIED MATHEMATICS

JOHN COLBURN ASSOCIATES
RELEASED BY COLBURN FILM DISTRIBUTORS

USES ANIMATION AND LIVE-ACTION PHOTOGRAPHY TO DESCRIBE
THE ELECTRONIC COMPUTER, ITS OPERATION, FUNCTIONS,
APPLICATIONS IN INDUSTRY AND COMMERCE, MATHEMATICAL
BASIS, AND THE BASIC UNITS OF WHICH IT IS COMPOSED.
BRIEFLY REVIEWS THE TYPES OF COMPUTERS AND SHOWS HOW
THE BINARY SYSTEM IS USED IN COMPUTERS. DISCUSSES
THE FUTURE OF COMPUTERS IN A COMPLEX SOCIETY, AND
INDICATES THE TYPES OF JOBS COMPUTERS CAN PERFORM.
WITH UTILIZATION GUIDE.

23 MIN., SD., COLOR, 16 MM.

UNIVERSITY OF CALIFORNIA	$10.00		5751
STATE UNIVERSITY OF IOWA	$5.00		U-5750
PENNSYLVANIA STATE UNIVERSITY	$4.75		621.8-17
UNIVERSITY OF COLORADO	$5.75	$8.50	NAME
INDIANA UNIVERSITY	$7.15		ISC-352

F0073   1961   CAB

INFORMATION RETRIEVAL

IBM
MADE BY NEWSFILM, USA

THE FIRST TWELVE MINUTES OF THE MOVIE DESCRIBES HOW A
THEORETICAL BUT TYPICAL LARGE COMPANY SOLVES ITS
COMMUNICATION PROBLEMS BY ADOPTING MODERN INFORMATION
RETRIEVAL PROCEDURES, USING CONVENTIONAL IBM DATA
PROCESSING SYSTEMS. DEALS WITH KWIC INDEXING, RESEARCH
PROJECT RETRIEVAL, DSI, DOCUMENT RETRIEVAL, SKILL INDEXING.

17 MIN., SD., COLOR, 16 MM.

IBM	FREE	NAME

F0074   1961   SCA

THE LIVING MACHINE. PARTS 1 AND 2

NATIONAL FILM BOARD OF CANADA

EXPLORATION OF PROGRESS IN ELECTRONICS TECHNOLOGY,
AND NEW FRONTIERS OF KNOWLEDGE AND EXPERIENCE, MAN-MADE
MACHINES WILL OPEN TO MAN HIMSELF. PART 1 DEMONSTATES
THE CAPACITIES OF ARTIFICIAL INTELLIGENCE. PART 2 SHOWS
EXPERIMENTS DUPLICATING ELECTRONICALLY SOME SENSORY
PERCEPTIONS. RAISES, THE QUESTION WHETHER WE SHALL ONE
DAY CREATE BEINGS SUPERIOR TO OURSELVES, WHO WILL SURVIVE
US ON EARTH. DRS. WARREN MCCULLOCK AND MARGARET MEAD
EXPRESS THEIR VIEWS.

60 MIN., SD., B/W, 16 MM.

PENNSYLVANIA STATE UNIVERSITY	$11.25	30547
NATIONAL FILM BOARD OF CANADA	$16.00	NAME
INDIANA UNIVERSITY	$9.40	CS-1513

F0075   1961   SCA

MAGNETIC MEMORY

MINNESOTA MINING AND MANUFACTURING CO.

EXPLAINS THAT MAGNETIC TAPE HAS ADDED A NEW DIMENSION
TO THE MEMORY OF MAN BY PROVIDING A NEW METHOD FOR
RECORDING AND PRESERVING THE KNOWLEDGE, SKILLS, AND
CREATIVE EFFORTS WHICH ARE VITAL INGREDIENTS OF BUSINESS.
OUTLINES THE MANY USES OF MAGNETIC TAPE. DESCRIBES THE
MANUFACTURING PROCESS, INCLUDES A DISCUSSION OF CONTROLS
EXERCISED TO PRODUCE TAPE.

25 MIN., SD., COLOR, 16 MM.

F0076   1961   JSCA

MATHEMATICAL PEEP SHOW

CHARLES EAMES
PURCHASE. CHARLES EAMES PRODUCTIONS $75.00

THIS FILM EXPLORES SEVERAL INTERESTING ASPECTS OF
MATHEMATICS - SYMMETRY, TOPOLOGY, THE WORLD OF NUMBERS,
FUNCTIONS AND THE METHOD USED BY ERATOSTHENES TO ESTABLISH
THE SIZE OF THE EARTH.

13 MIN., SD., COLOR, 16 MM.

IBM	FREE	NAME

F0077   1961   CA

MR. PUSH-A-BUTTON

U.S. NAVY DEPT.

SHOWS THE IMPORTANCE OF THE INDIVIDUAL MAN AND OF THE
CREWS OF SHIPS IN USING AUTOMATIC EQUIPMENT IN PUSH-BUTTON
WARFARE.

28 MIN., SD., COLOR, 16 MM.

U.S. NAVY	FREE	MN-9483

F0078   1961   CAB

THE NCR 390 ELECTRONIC DATA PROCESSOR

NATIONAL CASH REGISTER CO.

THIS FILM DESCRIBES THE NCR 390, A DIGITAL SOLID STATE
COMPUTER BUILT WITH MODULAR CONSTRUCTION. IT DEPICTS
THE FOUR METHODS OF INPUT AND OUTPUT, I.E. CONSOLE
KEYBOARD, PUNCHED PAPER TAPE, PUNCHED TAB CARDS, OR
EXTERNAL MAGNETIC MEMORY LEDGERS. THE FILM ALSO DESCRIBES
THE FUNCTIONING OF A MAGNETIC CORE MEMORY.

20 MIN., SD., COLOR, 16 MM.

NATIONAL CASH REGISTER CO.	FREE	NAME

F0079   1961   CA

THE NEXT STEP

DPD PROMOTIONAL SERVICES
PURCHASE. PRECISION FILM LABORATORIES, INC. $47.00

THIS FILM DESCRIBES THE IBM 1401 SYSTEMS APPLICATION
TO PUBLIC UTILITY ACCOUNTING AND PUBLIC UTILITY
ENGINEERING. IT TAKES THE VIEWER TO THE IBM DEMONSTRATION
BOOTH AT THE 1960 NATIONAL ACCOUNTING CONFERENCE FOR
PUBLIC UTILITY INDUSTRY FOR AN ON-THE-SPOT DEMONSTRATION
OF THE 1401 SYSTEM. SUITABLE FOR SALES PROMOTIONAL
PURPOSES.

15 MIN., SD., COLOR, 16 MM.

IBM   FREE   NAME

F0080   1961   CA

POTLACH FOREST, INC. PRESS CONFERENCE REPORT

NEWSFILM, USA
PURCHASE. GOTHAM FILM SERVICE $35.00

NEWS REPORT FILM DEMONSTRATING 1710 ON LINE TO A PAPER
MAKING MACHINE. EXECUTIVES OF POTLACH FOREST, INC. CITE
THEIR OBJECTIVES FOR INSTALLING THE 1710 AND THEIR
EXPECTATIONS. THIS FILM IS EXCELLENT CUSTOMER REFERENCE
OF THE FIRST 1710 INSTALLED IN THE PAPER INDUSTRY.

7 MIN., SD., B/W, 16 MM.

IBM   FREE   NAME

F0081   1961   SCA

THE PRINTED CIRCUIT STORY

BRAY STUDIOS, INC.
PURCHASE. BRAY STUDIOS, INC. $200.00

SHOWS COMPLETE MANUFACTURE OF PRINTED CIRCUITS AS WELL
AS RECOMMENDED TOOLS AND APPROVED REPAIR TECHNIQUES FOR
REPLACING COMPONENTS, SOLDERING, AND SERVICING OF PRINTED
WIRING.

25 MIN., SD., B/W, 16 MM.

PENNSYLVANIA STATE UNIVERSITY $9.00   30194
UNIVERSITY OF NEVADA $5.75 $8.50 NAME
BRAY STUDIOS, INC. $20.00   NAME

F0082   1961   CA

PROJECT SURE

DPD PROMOTIONAL SERVICES
PURCHASE. CAMPUS FILM PRODUCTIONS, INC. $165.00

THIS MOVIE IS A DETAILED DESCRIPTION OF THE SURE PROGRAM
GIVEN BY WAYNE HALL, MIDWESTERN REGION UTILITY
REPRESENTATIVE, TO THE AGA EEI CONVENTION IN NEW YORK
CITY. IN THE FIRST HALF, MR. HALL DESCRIBES THE PROGRAM.
THE SECOND HALF IS AN ACTUAL FILMED DEMONSTRATION OF THE
SURE PROGRAM RUNNING ON THE 7070. SUITABLE FOR IBM,
CUSTOMER AND PROSPECT AUDIENCES.

25 MIN., SD., COLOR, 16 MM.

IBM   FREE   NAME

F0083   1961   JSCA

THE QUESTION TREE

IBM CORP.
MADE BY HENRY STRAUSS PRODUCTIONS
PURCHASE. FILM AND TV NEWS ACTIVITIES DEPT., CHQ $50.00

AN EXAMINATION OF MAN'S AGE-OLD CURIOSITY CONCERNING
THE WORLD AROUND HIM, AND WHERE THIS CURIOSITY HAS LED
HIM. THE STORY OF HOW INTELLIGENT QUESTIONING LEADS TO
SCIENTIFIC DISCOVERY. INCLUDES SEQUENCES ON CRYOGENICS,
LANGUAGE TRANSLATION, VAPOR GROWTH AND OPTICAL MASER.

13 MIN., SD., COLOR, 16 MM., 35 MM.

IBM   FREE   NAME

F0084   1961   CA

THE REPORT GENERATOR

DPD PROMOTIONAL SERVICES
PURCHASE. PRECISION FILM LABORATORIES, INC. $35.00

DEMONSTRATES THE TECHNIQUES FOR USING FARGO AND RPG
REPORT GENERATING PROGRAMS FOR 1401 CARD SYSTEMS.
DEVELOPMENT OF THE SUBJECT IN THE FILM PARALLELS THE
FLIP CHART PRESENTATION, REPORT GENERATORS FOR THE 1401.
THESE FLIP CHARTS MAY BE USED TO REVIEW THE MATERIAL
AFTER SHOWING THE FILM.

9 MIN., SD., COLOR, 16 MM.

IBM   FREE   NAME

F0085   1961   CA

SDC'S AUTOMATED TEACHING PROJECT

SYSTEM DEVELOPMENT CORPORATION

DESIGNED AS AN INFORMAL INTERVIEW, THE FILM BRIEFS
VIEWERS ON THE NATURE AND POTENTIALS OF COMPUTER-ORIENTED
INSTRUCTION DEVELOPED AT SDC WITH A COMPLETE SYSTEM
APPROACH FOR ADMINISTRATORS, COUNSELORS, TEACHERS AND
STUDENTS. THE LENGTH AND DOWN-TO-EARTH TONE OF THE FILM
ENCOURAGE ITS USE FOR TELECASTS, CONVENTIONS AND DISCUSSIO
SESSIONS.

14 MIN., SD., COLOR, 16 MM.

SYSTEM DEVELOPMENT CORPORATION   FREE   F-37

F0086   1961   SCA

SDI...SELECTIVE DISSEMINATION OF INFORMATION

COMMUNICATIONS DEPT., ASDD
PURCHASE. PRECISION FILM LABORATORIES, INC. $16.00

DESCRIBES THE OPERATION OF SELECTIVE DISSEMINATION
OF INFORMATION WHICH IS CURRENTLY IN USE AT THE IBM
ADVANCED SYSTEMS DEVELOPMENT DIVISION AT THE MOHANSIC
LABORATORY. SUITABLE FOR EDUCATIONAL AND SALES PROMOTION
PURPOSES

5 MIN., SD., COLOR, 16 MM.

IBM   FREE   NAME

F0087   1961   CA

SPACE AGE ADMINISTRATION

REID H. RAY FILM INDUSTRIES
RELEASED BY RCA AND U.S. AIR FORCE RESERVE

THIS FILM SHOWS THE RCA 501 AT THE AIR FORCE RESERVE
RECORD CENTER TO KEEP RECORDS OF RESERVISTS. PORTRAYS
KEY ROLE OF ELECTRONIC DATA PROCESSING IN THE
ADMINISTRATIVE MANAGEMENT OF 500,000 RESERVISTS.

20 MIN., SD., COLOR, 16 MM.

RCA   FREE   NAME
U.S.A.F. FILM LIBRARY CENTER   FREE   SFP 1116

F0088   1961   CA

SUPERCONDUCTIVITY

IBM FEDERAL SYSTEMS DIV.
PURCHASE. DEPT. 415, IBM KINGSTON $60.00

THE PRINCIPLE OF SUPERCONDUCTIVITY AND THE FABRICATION
CYCLE OF SUPERCONDUCTIVE DEVICES ARE SHOWN IN A STEP-BY-
STEP SEQUENCE. A 135 CRYOTRON MEMORY PLANE, WHICH IS
THE DEVICE PRODUCED, CAN ACTUALLY BE SEEN TAKING FORM.
EXCELLENT TIME LAPSE PHOTOGRAPHY GRAPHICALLY SHOWS THE
EVAPORATION OF THIN FILM LAYERS ON A GLASS SUBSTRATE
TO MAKE THE MEMORY PLANE.

10 MIN., SD., COLOR, 16 MM.

IBM   FREE   NAME

F0089   1961   SCA

THEN AND NOW

UNIVAC

AN ACCOUNT OF THE DEVELOPMENT OF ENIAC, THE FIRST
ELECTRONIC COMPUTER, BY J. PRESPER ECKERT AND DR. JOHN
W. MAUCHLY, CO-INVENTORS OF THE SYSTEM. FOLLOWING THEIR
ACCOUNT OF ENIAC, MR. ECKERT AND DR. MAUCHLY DISCUSS
THEIR CURRENT INTERESTS AND ACTIVITIES.

12 MIN., SD., COLOR, 16 MM.

UNIVAC DIV., SPERRY RAND CORP.   FREE   NAME

F0090   1961   CA

TEACHING MACHINES. PART 1 OF 2

UNIVERSITY OF WASHINGTON

DESCRIBES CONCEPTS OF AUTOMATED TEACHING MACHINES
EDUCATORS HAVE SHOWN A MARKED INTEREST IN TEACHING
MACHINES IN THEIR RESPECTIVE FIELDS, AND THIS FILM
EXPLAINS SOME OF THESE INVESTIGATIONS IN THE PAST FEW
YEARS.

30 MIN., SD., B/W, 16 MM.

STATE UNIVERSITY OF IOWA $4.50   U-5524
UNIVERSITY OF WASHINGTON $7.50   NAME

F0091   1961   CA

TEACHING MACHINES. PART 2 OF 2

UNIVERSITY OF WASHINGTON

PROGRAMMING FOR TEACHING MACHINES SHOWS THE CONSTRUCTION
OF ITEMS IN ORDER TO INSURE THE CORRECT RESPONSE, THE
UTILIZATION OF PROMPTING, CONFIRMATION, AND SIZE OF THE
ITEMS TO BE USED. IN ADDITION, SUCH VARIABLES AS THE
MODE OF RESPONSE AND THE USE OF BRANCHING PROGRAMS HAVE
YET TO BE DEFINITELY AND SYSTEMATICALLY INVESTIGATED.

30 MIN., SD., B/W, 16 MM.

STATE UNIVERSITY OF IOWA $4.50   U-5525
UNIVERSITY OF WASHINGTON $7.50   NAME

F0092   1961   SCA

THE TYRANNY OF LARGE NUMBERS

WESTERN ELECTRIC COMPANY
MADE BY PELICAN FILMS

FOLLOWS THE WORK OF WESTERN ELECTRIC ENGINEERS IN
DEVELOPING A PROCESS FOR THE MANUFACTURE OF CARBON
DEPOSITED RESISTORS IN LARGE QUANTITIES ACCORDING TO
THE RIGID ELECTRICAL SPECIFICATIONS. SHOWS THE OPERATION
OF THE BLOCK-LONG COMPUTER CONTROLLED PRODUCTION LINE
AND EXPLAINS HOW THE BRAIN OF THE PRODUCTION LINE IS
EMPLOYED TO PROGRAM PRODUCTION CONTROL, PROVIDE INITIAL
SET-UP INFORMATION, DETER DRIFTS, AND INSTITUTE
CORRECTIVE ACTION.

16 MIN., SD., COLOR, 16 MM

WESTERN ELECTRIC   FREE   NAME

F0093   1961   SCA

A VOICE FOR MERCURY

AMERICAN TELEPHONE AND TELEGRAPH CO.
MADE BY AUDIO PRODUCTIONS

THIS FILM PRESENTS A COMPLETE STORY OF A SPACE SHOT
FROM THE TRAINING OF AN ASTRONAUT TO THE VAST PREPARATIONS
AND ACTIVITY BY GROUND COMMUNICATIONS PEOPLE AROUND
THE GLOBE. IT DESCRIBES HOW A GLOBE-CIRCLING TRACKING
AND COMMUNICATIONS NETWORK MONITORS, GUIDES AND
COMMUNICATES WITH MAN IN SPACE. CENTRALIZED COMPUTERS
CALCULATE ORBITAL DATA AS THE SHOT CIRCLES THE GLOBE
AT BREATHTAKING SPEED. YOU CAN INCREASE YOUR KNOWLEDGE
OF THE SPACE AGE BY SEEING THIS FILM.

15 MIN., SD., COLOR, 16 MM.

NASA   FREE   NAME
WESTERN ELECTRIC   FREE
ASSOCIATION FILMS, INC.   FREE   S-830

F0094   1961   SCA

WHAT IS EDP. (PRINCIPLES OF EDP)

DPD PROMOTIONAL SERVICES
PURCHASE. PICTORIAL PRESENTATION OF AMERICA, INC. $85.00

DISCUSSION OF THE BASIC PRINCIPLES OF ELECTRONIC DATA
PROCESSING. EXPLAINS INPUT, STORAGE, PROCESSING AND
OUTPUT OF DATA. DEALS BRIEFLY WITH PUNCHED CARDS,
PAPER AND MAGNETIC TAPE, MAGNETIC INK, AND MAGNETIC
DRUM, DISK AND TAPE STORAGE.

13 MIN., SD., COLOR, 16 MM.

IBM   FREE   NAME

F0095   1962   SCA

ACROSS THE WORLD IN THREE SECONDS

SIDNEY STIBER PRODUCTIONS
PURCHASE. IDEAL PICTURES

DESCRIBES, IN GENERAL TERMS, THE WORLD-WIDE PASSENGER
AND CARGO RESERVATIONS NETWORK OF PAN AMERICAN AIRWAYS
AND HOW IT WILL BE ENHANCED BY AN ADVANCED IBM
TELEPROCESSING SYSTEM. THIS MAJOR DEVELOPMENT WILL
BRING ELECTRONIC SPEEDS, ACCURACY AND EFFICIENCY TO
AIRLINE RESERVATIONS.

13 MIN., SD., COLOR, 16 MM.

IBM   FREE   NAME
IDEAL PICTURES $2.50   NAME

F0096   1962   CA

AUTONETICS IN ACTION

NORTH AMERICAN AVIATION

THIS FILM TAKES YOU INTO A VARIETY OF AUTONETICS' MAJOR
CONTRIBUTIONS, INERTIAL NAVIGATION SYSTEMS FOR POLARIS-
CARRYING SUBMARINES, GUIDANCE AND FLIGHT CONTROL FOR
MINUTEMEN INTERCONTINENTAL BALLISTIC MISSILE, BOMBING-
NAVIGATION SYSTEMS FOR A5C BOMBER AIRCRAFT, ARMAMENT
CONTROL FOR F-104 AND F-105 COMBAT SUPPORT AIRCRAFT,
AND COMPÚTER AND DATA SYSTEMS.

18 MIN., SD., COLOR, 16 MM.

AUTONETICS DIVISION   FREE   AMP 449-1962

F0097   1962   C B

THE BANK

DPD PROMOTIONAL SERVICES
PURCHASE. PRECISION FILM LABORATORIES, INC. $58.00

A DETAILED PRESENTATION OF DEMAND DEPOSIT ACCOUNTING,
INCLUDING DEMONSTRATIONS ON THE 1401 DATA PROCESSING
SYSTEM, 1201 PROOF INSCRIBER AND 1203 UNIT INSCRIBER,
AND SHOWING ALL ACCOUNTING MANAGEMENT REPORTS. BEST
SUITED TO AUDIENCES WITH SOME KNOWLEDGE OF BANKING
APPLICATIONS.

19 MIN., SD., COLOR, 16 MM.

IBM   FREE   NAME

F0098   1962   JSCA

BEFORE SATURN

GEORGE C. MARSHALL SPACE FLIGHT CENTER

A HISTORY OF THE DEVELOPMENT OF ROCKETS FROM THE EARLY
CHINESE THROUGH THE SATRUN LAUNCH BOOSTER.

15 MIN., SD., COLOR, 16 MM.

F0099   1962   SCA

BY THE NUMBERS

FEDERAL SYSTEMS DIVISION, IBM
PURCHASE. DEPT. 415, KINGSTON $90.00

THE STORY OF HOW VISUAL IMAGES ARE CONVERTED INTO
NUMBERS SO THAT THEY CAN BE INTERPRETED BY COMPUTERS.

DESCRIBES THE APPLICATION OF CONVERTING AERIAL
PHOTOGRAPHS INTO DETAILED MAPS BY USING IMAGE PROCESSING
TECHNOLOGY.

16 MIN., SD., COLOR, 16 MM.

| IBM | FREE | NAME |

F0100   1962   SCA

CAREERS IN BUSINESS DATA PROCESSING

ORANGE COAST COLLEGE
MADE AND RELEASED BY UNI. OF SOUTHERN CALIFORNIA

DESCRIBES OPPORTUNITIES FOR CAREERS IN DATA PROCESSING
IN BUSINESS. USES ANIMATED GRAPHICS AND LIVE ACTION TO
POINT OUT THE NEED FOR MORE EFFICIENT PROCEDURES IN THE
HANDLING OF DATA IN TODAY'S COMPLEX BUSINESS WORLD AND
THE VALUE OF THE BASIC ELEMENTS OF COMPUTERS. SUGGESTS
A CURRICULUM IN BUSINESS DATA PROCESSING.

13 MIN., SD., COLOR, 16 MM.

F0101   1962   SCA

THE CHALLENGE OF CHANGE

NATIONAL EDUCATIONAL TELEVISION AND RADIO CENTER
MADE BY LOUIS DE ROCHMONT ASSOCIATES
PURCHASE. FILM AND TV NEWS ACTIVITIES, CHQ

DEPICTS THE VALUE OF COUNSELING IN HELPING YOUTH TO
PREPARE FOR AN ERA OF TECHNOLOGICAL CHANGE. THE FILM,
SUPPORTED FINANCIALLY BY IBM, WAS MADE FOR THE NATIONAL
EDUCATIONAL TELEVISION NETWORK (NET) AND THE U.S. OFFICE
OF EDUCATION. UNDER THE AUSPICES OF A NATIONAL ADVISORY
COUNCIL OF LEADERS IN GUIDANCE COUNSELING, THE LATEST
TECHNIQUES IN GUIDANCE AND COUNSELOR TRAINING ARE
SHOWN, WITH SPECIAL EMPHASIS ON HELPING STUDENTS PREPARE
FOR THE WORK WORLD OF TOMORROW. WITH VIEWERS GUIDE.

28 MIN., SD., COLOR, 16 MM.

| IBM | FREE | NAME |

F0102   1962   C B

COMPUTER CONTROL OF A CATALYTIC CRACKER

ALLEND'OR PRODUCTIONS
PURCHASE. ALLEND'OR PRODUCTIONS $73.00

SHOWS AN IBM CONTROL SYSTEM, ON-LINE TO THE STANDARD
OIL COMPANY OF CALIFORNIA'S PETROLEUM CATALYTIC CRACKING
UNIT AT EL SEGUNDO, CALIFORNIA, PERFORMING CLOSED-LOOP
OPERATIONS. IT OUTLINES CONTROL PROBLEMS AND DEMONSTRATES
HOW IBM CONTROL SYSTEMS SOLVE THEM. BEST SUITED FOR
AUDIENCES FAMILIAR WITH THE PETROLEUM PROCESSES INVOLVED.

9 MIN., SD., COLOR, 16 MM.

| IBM | FREE | NAME |

F0103   1962   CAB

COMPUTER PROGRAMMING FOR N/C MACHINES

IBM CORP., DATA PROCESSING DIV.
PURCHASE. TRAINING FILMS, INC.

THIS MOVIE ENCOMPASSES THE AUTOSPOT AND AUTOMAP PROGRAMS.
BOTH AUTOSPOT, FOR POINT-TO-POINT POSITIONING, AND
AUTOMAP, FOR CONTOUR MACHINERY, ARE DESCRIBED IN DETAIL.
MACHINE EXAMPLES, PROGRAM FEATURES, AND INHERENT ADVANTAGES
ARE AMONG THE HIGHLIGHTS.

15 MIN., SD., COLOR, 16 MM.

| IBM | FREE | NAME |

F0104   1962   CAB

THE CONTROL REVOLUTION. (THE COMPUTER AND THE MIND OF MAN)
NET FILM SERVICE

KQED TV, SAN FRANCISCO, CALIFORNIA
PURCHASE. FILM AND TV NEWS ACTIVITIES, CHQ

THIS MOVIE SHOWS ONE OF THE EARLIEST NON-SCIENTIFIC
APPLICATIONS OF COMPUTER CONTROL, THE RECORDING, STORING
AND PROCESSING OF VAST DATA HANDLED BY THE SOCIAL SECURITY
ADMINISTRATION. JOHN MCCARTHY, DIRECTOR OF DATA PROCESSING

AT WYMAN GORDON COMPANY DESCRIBES HOW AN INDUSTRIAL PLANT
USES A COMPUTER TO KEEP TRACK OF AND TO INTEGRATE
INFORMATION. AT THE NUMERICAL MACHINING CORPORATION,
COMPUTERS TOOL DELICATE MACHINE PARTS. AT STANDARD OIL
REFINERY, A COMPUTER CONTROL SYSTEM IS USED TO ACHIEVE
CONTINUOUS AND AUTOMATIC PROCESS CONTROL. EXPERTS COMMENT
ON RELEASING MANAGEMENT FROM ROUTINE DECISION-MAKING SO
ATTENTION CAN BE FOCUSED ON MORE DIFFICULT PROBLEMS.

30 MIN., SD., B/W, 16 MM.

NATIONAL EDUCATIONAL TELEVISION		NAME
N.E.T. FILM SERVICE		NAME
IBM	FREE	NAME
INDIANA UNIVERSITY	$5.40	BS-90

F0105   1962   CAB

DESIGN AUTOMATION AT IBM

IBM CORP.
PURCHASE. TRAINING FILMS, INC.

THIS DYNAMIC MOVIE FEATURES THE DESIGN AUTOMATION SYSTEM
CURRENTLY EMPLOYED AT THE IBM ENDICOTT AND POUGHKEEPSIE
PLANTS. IT HIGHLIGHTS THE USE OF AN IBM DATA PROCESSING
SYSTEM AS AN AID FOR ENGINEERING COMPUTER DESIGN AND
NUMERICAL CONTROL OF PRODUCTION TOOLS.

18 MIN., SD., COLOR, 16 MM.

| IBM | FREE | NAME |

F0106   1962   CA

DIGITAL COMPUTER TECHNIQUES - BINARY NUMBERS

U.S. DEPT. OF NAVY

AN EXPLANATION BY MEANS OF ANIMATION OF THE BINARY SYSTEM
IN CONTRAST TO THE DECIMAL SYSTEM OF MATHEMATICS. EXPLAINS
HOW BINARY NUMBERS ARE CONSTRUCTED AND HOW ARITHMETICAL
OPERATIONS ARE PERFORMED WITH THEM.

13 MIN., SD., COLOR, 16 MM.

| U.S. NAVY | FREE | MN-8969-B |

F0107   1952   CA

DIGITAL COMPUTER TECHNIQUES - COMPUTER UNITS

U.S. DEPT. OF NAVY

AN INTRODUCTION TO THE FIVE MAJOR UNITS OF A DIGITAL
COMPUTER. DESCRIBES THE INPUT UNIT AND HOW IT READS THE
PROBLEM DATA AND INSTRUCTIONS, THE OUTPUT UNIT AND HOW IT
DELIVERS PROBLEM SOLUTIONS IN SOME FORM OF OUTPUT MEDIUM,
THE ARITHMETIC UNIT, ITS COMPOSITION AND EXAMPLES OF HOW
ITS BASIC COMPONENTS WORK, THE CONTROL UNIT AND THE
PURPOSES OF SEQUENCING, CLOCKING, AND TIMING.

24 MIN., SD., COLOR, 16 MM.

| U.S. NAVY | FREE | MN-8969-D |

F0108   1962   CA

DIGITAL COMPUTER TECHNIQUES - INTRODUCTION

U.S. DEPT. OF NAVY

A GENERAL INTRODUCTION TO DIGITAL COMPUTERS, THE
HISTORICAL ORIGINS OF CALCULATING DEVICES, THE DIFFERENCES
BETWEEN ANALOG AND DIGITAL COMPUTERS AND THE PRINCIPAL
STEPS IN DIGITAL COMPUTER SOLUTIONS OF PROBLEMS.

16 MIN., SD., COLOR, 16 MM.

| U.S. NAVY | FREE | MN-8969-A |

F0109   1962   CA

DIGITAL COMPUTER TECHNIQUES - LOGIC ELEMENT CIRCUITS

U.S. DEPT. OF NAVY

ILLUSTRATES HOW SOLID STATE ELECTRONICS ARE USED IN
MODERN COMPUTERS. SHOWS DIAGRAMS FOR DIODE, CIRCUITS,
THE P-N-P TRANSISTOR, ITS USE IN AND, OR, NOR, INVERTER,
AND FLIP-FLOP GATE. SHOWS HOW THE CIRCUITS HANDLE THE
INPUT SIGNALS OF HIGH AND/OR LOW VOLTAGES REPRESENTING

BINARY ONES AND BINARY ZEROS RESPECTIVELY, AND HOW THE
PROPER OUTPUT SIGNAL IS PRODUCED.

16 MIN., SD., COLOR, 16 MM.

U.S. NAVY   FREE   MN-8969-E

FO110   1962   CA

DIGITAL COMPUTER TECHNOLOGY —LOGIC SYMBOLOGY

U.S. DEPT. OF NAVY

SHOWS THE BASIC U.S. MILITARY STANDARD SYMBOLS FOR THE
LOGIC ELEMENTS OF COMPUTERS AS AN INTRODUCTION TO DIGITAL
COMPUTER LOGIC SYMBOLOGY. THE LOGIC ELEMENTS, AND, OR, OR
(EXCLUSIVE), NOR DELAY, INVERTER, FLIP-FLOP AND THE WAY
THEY FUNCTION IN HANDLING ELECTRONIC SIGNALS ARE SHOWN
IN ART.

15 MIN., SD., COLOR, 16 MM.

U.S. NAVY   FREE   MN-8969-C

FO111   1962   CA

DIGITAL COMPUTER TECHNOLOGY — PROGRAMMING

U.S. DEPT. OF NAVY

DEFINES COMPUTER PROGRAMMING, EXPLAINS WHAT IS MEANT BY
ANALYZING THE PROBLEM. SHOWS HOW A SIMPLE FLOW CHART IS
PREPARED WITH SYMBOLS GIVING THEIR MEANING. SHOWS BY USE
OF A SINGLE EXAMPLE HOW INSTRUCTIONS TO THE COMPUTER ARE
ENCODED IN COMPUTER LANGUAGE.

14 MIN., SD., COLOR, 16 MM.

U.S. NAVY   FREE   MN-8969-F

FO112   1962   CAB

EDP FOR YOUR PAYROLL

BANK OF AMERICA

EDP FOR YOUR PAYROLL INTRODUCES A TIME-AND-MONEY-SAVING
MIRACLE TO THOSE UNFAMILIAR WITH ELECTRONIC DATA PROCESSING
AND EXPLAINS BOTH THE PAYROLL SERVICE PLAN AND ITS BENEFITS
TO LARGE AND SMALL BUSINESS. THE FILM SHOWS HOW TO SPEED
UP THE PAYING OUT AND RECORDING OF SALARY CHECKS AND HOW
TO PROVIDE CONTROLLING INDICATORS.

14 MIN., SD., COLOR, 16 MM.

BANK OF AMERICA   FREE   NAME

FO113   1962   CAB

ENGINE AT THE DOOR. (THE COMPUTER AND THE MIND OF MAN)

KQED TV, SAN FRANCISCO, CALIFORNIA
RELEASED BY N.E.T. FILM SERVICE
PURCHASE. FILM AND TV NEWS ACTIVITIES, CHQ

J. PRESPER ECKERT, CO-INVENTOR OF ENIAC AND VICE-
PRESIDENT OF UNIVAC DIVISION OF THE SPERRY RAND
CORPORATION, POSES THE QUESTION, WILL MACHINES EVER
RUN MAN. ERNEST NAGEL, PROFESSOR OF PHILOSOPHY AT
COLUMBIA UNIVERSITY, AND DR. C.R. DECARLO, DIRECTOR
OF EDUCATION FOR IBM, DISCUSS THE USES MAN MAKES OF
SCIENCE AND TECHNOLOGY TODAY AND POINT OUT MAN'S
RESPONSIBILITY FOR THE WISE AND BENEFICIAL USE OF
SCIENCE AND THE INSTRUMENTS OF TECHNOLOGY AS A MEANS
TO A BETTER LIFE.

30 MIN., SD., B/W, 16 MM.

NATIONAL EDUCATIONAL TELEVISION   NAME
N.E.T. FILM SERVICE   NAME
IBM   FREE   NAME
INDIANA UNIVERSITY $5.40   BS-92

FO114   1962   CA

THE FIRST ALERT

BURROUGHS CORPORATION

DAY AND NIGHT, RADAR PICKET PLANES PATROL OUR COASTLINES.
SHOULD AN AIRBORNE ATTACK BE LAUNCHED AGAINST US, THESE
PICKET PLANES WILL NOTIFY THE MAINLINE. A COMPACT

COMPUTER SYSTEM BUILT BY BURROUGHS IS THE HEART OF THIS
SYSTEM. THIS IS THE STORY OF THE SYSTEM.

15 MIN., SD., COLOR, 16 MM.

BURROUGHS CORPORATION   FREE   NAME

FO115   1962   JSCA

HIGHWAY TO INFINITY

BURROUGHS CORPORATION

AN EXPOSITION OF THE COMPUTER BACKUP NECESSARY FOR SPACE
FLIGHT. DOCUMENTED ON BURROUGHS AND NASA FILM FOOTAGE
IS JOHN GLENN'S FLIGHT FROM BLAST-OFF, THROUGH ORBITAL
STAGE, INTO DANGEROUS RE-ENTRY, BACK TO EARTH.

18 MIN., SD., COLOR, 16 MM.

BURROUGHS CORPORATION   FREE   NAME

FO116   1962   C B

IBM CONTROL SYSTEMS AT WORK

NEWSFILM, USA
PURCHASE. NEWSFILM, USA $12.00

IBM CONTROL SYSTEMS ARE SHOWN GUIDING A FRACTIONAL
DISTILLATION UNIT AT THE AMERICAN OIL COMPANY IN WHITING,
INDIANA, AND A BLAST FURNACE OPERATION AT THE INLAND
STEEL COMPANY OF HAMMOND, INDIANA. THE FILM REVIEWS
PROCESS CONTROL PROBLEMS, AND DEMONSTRATES HOW IBM
CONTROL SYSTEMS HELP TO SOLVE THESE PROBLEMS. BEST
SUITED FOR AUDIENCES WITH A KNOWLEDGE OF INDUSTRIAL
PROCESS CONTROL.

5 MIN., SD., B/W, 16 MM.

IBM   FREE   NAME

FO117   1962   CA

THE IBM 1404 PRINTER

IBM
PURCHASE. MOTION PICTURES

FILM DESCRIBES FUNCTIONAL PRINCIPLES OF THE 1404 CHAIN
PRINTER FOR THE 1401 DATA PROCESSING SYSTEM. INCLUDED
ARE SUGGESTED APPLICATION AREAS FOR CUT CARD FORMS WHICH
THE 1404 PRINTER IS ABLE TO PRINT ON BECAUSE OF ITS BILL
FEED CAPACITY.

8 MIN., SD., COLOR, 16 MM.

IBM   FREE   NAME

FO118   1962   CA

THE IBM 1440 DATA PROCESSING SYSTEM

IBM
PURCHASE. MOTION PICTURES

THIS FILM DESCRIBES THE 1440 DATA PROCESSING SYSTEM
AND ITS APPLICATION TO SMALL BUSINESSES.

48 MIN., SD., B/W, 16 MM.

IBM   FREE   NAME

FO119   1962   CAB

INTERIOR BALLISTICS COMPUTER PROGRAM

AEROJET GENERAL CORPORATION

THIS FILM SHOWS HOW THE PROGRAM IS PROCESSED AND HOW
ENGINEERS ANALYZE AND USE INFORMATION.

19 MIN., SD., COLOR, 16 MM.

AEROJET GENERAL CORP.   FREE   NAME

F0120   1962   CA

INSURANCE BULLETIN NO. 1

DPD PROMOTIONAL SERVICES
PURCHASE. PRECISION FILM LABORATORIES, INC. $38.00

AN INFORMATION HANDLING REVOLUTION IS TAKING PLACE
WITHIN THE INSURANCE INDUSTRY. THIS PICTURE REPORT IS
DESIGNED TO KEEP YOU ABREAST OF NEW TECHNIQUES UTILIZING
RANDOM ACCESS MEMORY AND REMOTE INQUIRY STATIONS TO MAKE
POLICY INFORMATION INSTANTLY AVAILABLE TO ALL DEPARTMENTS
NEEDING IT. IT IS NARRATED BY IBM INDUSTRY REPRESENTATIVES
WHO DESCRIBE THE FEATURES AND BENEFITS OF THE INSURANCE
INFORMATION SYSTEM AND SHOWS A DEMONSTRATION OF THE IBM
1014 REMOTE INQUIRY STATION.

12 MIN., SD., COLOR, 16 MM.

IBM   FREE   NAME

F0121   1962   CA

LOGIC BY MACHINE. (THE COMPUTER AND THE MIND OF MAN)

KQED TV, SAN FRANCISCO, CALIFORNIA
RELEASED BY N.E.T. FILM SERVICE
PURCHASE. FILM AND TV NEWS ACTIVITIES, CHQ

A BASIC INTRODUCTION TO COMPUTERS. DR. RICHARD C.
HAMMING, RESEARCH MATHEMATICIAN AT BELL TELEPHONE
LABORATORIES, DISCUSSES THE COMPUTER REVOLUTION. DR.
ERNEST NAGEL, LEADING LOGICIAN AND PHILOSOPHER AT
COLUMBIA UNIVERSITY, TALKS ABOUT THE RELATIONSHIP OF
MAN AND MACHINE AND THE RELATIONSHIP OF THE SYMBOLIC
WORLD OF MATHEMATICS TO THE REAL WORLD OF OBJECTS AND
EVENTS

30 MIN., SD., B/W, 16 MM.

NATIONAL EDUCATIONAL TELEVISION   NAME
N.E.T. FILM SERVICE   NAME
IBM   FREE   NAME
INDIANA UNIVERSITY $5.40   BS-87

F0122   1962   CA

MANAGERS AND MODELS. (THE COMPUTER AND THE MIND OF MAN)

KQED TV, SAN FRANCISCO, CALIFORNIA
RELEASED BY N.E.T. FILM SERVICE
PURCHASE. FILM AND TV NEWS ACTIVITIES, CHQ

DESIGN AND SIMULATION CAPABILITIES OF THE MODERN COMPUTER
ARE EXPLORED. THE IMPORTANCE OF MATHEMATICAL MODELS IN
THE TRANSLATION OF A MODEL OF A SATURN ROCKET INTO
NUMERICAL TERMS, AND THE PLACE OF COMPUTERS IN THE
DESIGN AND TESTING OF THE BOOSTER STAGE IS DISCUSSED.
A COMPUTER IS USED TO SELECT THE OPTIMUM DESIGN FOR A
CHEMICAL PLANT, A MATHEMATICAL SIMULATION OF A REFINING
PROCESS IS ILLUSTRATED. THE VALUE TO MANAGEMENT OF A
COMPUTER SIMULATION MODEL IS DISCUSSED. THIS MOVIE IS
EXCELLENT FOR CUSTOMER AND PROSPECT PRESENTATION.

30 MIN., SD., B/W, 16 MM.

NATIONAL EDUCATIONAL TELEVISION   NAME
N.E.T. FILM SERVICE
IBM   FREE   NAME
INDIANA UNIVERSITY $5.40   BS-91

F0123   1962   SCA

MOBIDIC JOINS THE FIELD ARMY

U.S. DEPT. OF ARMY

THE STORY OF THE DEVELOPMENT, APPLICATION AND OPERATION
OF MOBIDIC, THE FIRST LARGE SCALE COMPUTER DISIGNED FOR
FIELD USE.

16 MIN., SD., COLOR, 16 MM.

U.S. ARMY   FREE   NAME

F0124   1962   JSCA

OAO...EYE IN SPACE

WILLIAM BERNAL
PURCHASE. FILM AND TV NEWS ACTIVITIES $25.00

THROUGH COLORFUL ANIMATION AND A STRIKING MUSICAL SCORE,
THIS FILM TELLS THE STORY OF THE ORBITING ASTRONOMICAL
OBSERVATORY. A TELESCOPE IN SPACE, GATHERING INFORMATION
TO BE PROCESSED BY COMPUTERS ON EARTH. MISSION, TO

UNVEIL THE MYSTERIES OF THE UNIVERSE THROUGH ULTRAVIOLET
MAPPING OF THE STARS.

8 MIN., SD., COLOR, 16 MM., 35 MM.

IBM   FREE   NAME

F0125   1962   CAB

PERT COST

MANAGEMENT SYSTEMS CORPORATION AND U.S. NAVY
PURCHASE. MANAGEMENT SYSTEMS CORPORATION

DISCUSSES THE PRINCIPLES OF PERT COST AND HOW TO APPLY
THEM. DEMONSTRATES THE PLANNING AND CONTROL FRAMEWORK
OF THE WORK BREAKDOWN, THE PROJECT NETWORK, AND THE
ACCOUNT CODE STRUCTURE TO GENERATE INTEGRATED TIME AND
COST STATUS, SHOWS EXAMPLES OF INFORMATION GENERATED BY
COMPUTER PRINTOUTS, SUMMARY REPORTS, AND GRAPHIC DISPLAYS.

27 MIN., SD., COLOR, 16 MM.

INDUSTRIAL EDUCATION FILMS, INC. $50.00/5 DAYS   NAME
IBM   FREE   NAME

F0126   1962   CA

RANDOM EVENTS

EDUCATIONAL SERVICES
RELEASED BY MODERN TALKING PICTURE SERVICE

PROFESSOR DONALD IVEY AND PATTERSON HUME SHOW HOW THE
OVER-ALL EFFECT OF A VERY LARGE NUMBER OF RANDOM EVENTS
CAN BE VERY PREDICTABLE, USING SEVERAL UNUSUAL GAMES TO
BRING OUT THE STATISTICAL NATURE OF THIS PREDICTABLE
NATURE OF RADIOACTIVE DECAY IN TERMS OF WHAT IS KNOWN.

33 MIN., SD., B/W, 16 MM.

PENNSYLVANIA STATE UNIVERSITY $6.25   30287

F0127   1962   CA

SKETCHPAD

M.I.T.. ELECTRONIC SYSTEMS LAB

AN APPLICATION OF THE TX-2 COMPUTER, USING A LIGHT
PEN DRAWING LANGUAGE WHICH PERMITS ARBITRARY PICTURE
ELEMENTS FROM PREVIOUSLY DEFINED SHAPES.

7 MIN., SD., B/W

ELECTRONIC SYSTEMS LABORATORY   FREE   NAME

F0128   1962   CA

TOMORROW

UNITED CHURCH OF CHRIST
PURCHASE. UNITED CHURCH OF CHRIST $160.00
PURCHASE. ASSOCIATION FILMS, INC. $160.00

THIS FILM IS DESIGNED TO MAKE PEOPLE THINK ABOUT AND
DISCUSS THE EFFECTS OF AUTOMATION ON OUR SOCIETY. THE
ATTITUDES OF BOTH MANAGEMENT AND LABOR ARE EXPRESSED
IN AN IMPARTIAL ATMOSPHERE. AS FAR AS WE KNOW, THIS
IS THE FIRST FILM DISCUSSION IN DEPTH OF THE ETHICS
INVOLVED IN THE PROBLEMS OF AUTOMATION AND EFFECTS
ON THE PEOPLE INVOLVED.

30 MIN., SD., B/W, 16 MM.

UNIVERSITY OF CALIFORNIA $9.00   5807
UNITED CHURCH OF CHRIST $8.00   NAME
ASSOCIATION FILMS, INC. $8.00   CC-504

F0129   1962   CAB

TRANSIT BANKING TODAY

IBM CORPORATION
PURCHASE. TRAINING FILMS, INC.

THIS FILM DESCRIBES A NEW APPROACH TO TRANSIT OPERATIONS
WITH THE HIGH SPEED 1419 ON-LINE WITH THE 1401 AND
FEATURING THE NEW AND VERSATILE SELECTIVE TAPE LISTING
DEVICE ON THE 1403 PRINTER. THE VIEWER IS TAKEN THROUGH
THE ENTIRE CHECK PROCESSING PROCEDURE WHICH CLOSES A
COMPLETELY AUTOMATED LEEP OF IBM BANK DATA PROCESSING
SERVICES, FROM ENCODING OF AMOUNTS ON THE 1203 THROUGH

TRANSIT TO DEMAND DEPOSIT ACCOUNTING. OTHER BANK
APPLICATIONS ARE STATED AS EQUALLY ADAPTABLE TO THE SYSTEM.

10 MIN., SD., COLOR, 16 MM.

IBM   FREE   NAME

COVERS BOTH THE FUNCTIONS AND USE OF THE IBM 1428 IN A
CLEAR, EASY-TO-UNDERSTAND MANNER.

11 MIN., SD., COLOR, 16 MM.

IBM   FREE   NAME

F0130   1962   CA

UNIVERSAL MACHINE. (THE COMPUTER AND THE MIND OF MAN)

KQED TV, SAN FRANCISCO, CALIFORNIA
RELEASED BY N.E.T. FILM SERVICE
PURCHASE. FILM AND TV NEWS ACTIVITIES, CHQ

WHY THE COMPUTER CAN BE CALLED A UNIVERSAL MACHINE.
DR. C.R. DECARLO, DIRECTOR OF EDUCATION FOR IBM, COMMENTS
ON THE COMPUTER REVOLUTION. INTRODUCTION TO PROGRAMMING
LANGUAGES SUCH AS FORTRAN, FLOW-MATIC, AND ALGOL.
DISTINGUISHED EXPERTS DISCUSS FUTURE METHODS OF USING
COMPUTERS.

30 MIN., SD., B/W, 16 MM.

NATIONAL EDUCATIONAL TELEVISION		NAME
N.E.T. FILM SERVICE		NAME
IBM	FREE	NAME
INDIANA UNIVERSITY	$5.40	BS-89

F0131   1962   CA

UNIVERSE OF NUMBERS. (THE COMPUTER AND THE MIND OF MAN)

KQED TV, SAN FRANCISCO, CALIFORNIA
RELEASED BY N.E.T. FILM SERVICE
PURCHASE. FILM AND TV NEWS ACTIVITIES, CHQ

THE HISTORY OF COMPUTER DEVELOPMENT FROM THE FIRST
MECHANICAL CALCULATOR INVENTED BY BLAISE PASCAL IN THE
17TH CENTURY TO ENIAC, THE FIRST COMPLETELY ELECTRONIC
CALCULATOR BUILT IN THE MID-1940'S BY JOHN MAUCHLY AND
J. PRESPER ECKERT. MR. ECKERT, VICE-PRESIDENT OF UNIVAC
DIVISION OF SPERRY RAND CORPORATION, DESCRIBES THE
CONSTRUCTION OF THE MATHEMATICAL MACHINE. FRED GRUENBERGER
OF THE RAND CORPORATION SHOWS DR. RICHARD HAMMING HOW HE
TRAINS YOUNG PEOPLE IN COMPUTER TECHNOLOGY.

30 MIN., SD., B/W, 16 MM.

NATIONAL EDUCATIONAL TELEVISION		NAME
N.E.T. FILM SERVICE		NAME
IBM	FREE	NAME
INDIANA UNIVERSITY	$5.40	BS-88

F0132   1962   CA

YOUR AIR WEATHER SERVICE

U.S. DEPT. OF AIR FORCE

PICTURES OPERATION OF GLOBAL AIR WEATHER SERVICE AND
POINTS OUT ITS CAPABILITIES AND LIMITATIONS. PORTRAYS
AWS CONTROL CENTER AS SAC COMMAND POST WHERE WORLDWIDE
WEATHER CONDITIONS ARE GATHERED, COMPUTER PROCESSED AND
TRANSMITTED TO SUBORDINATE WEATHER UNITS.

30 MIN., SD., COLOR, 16 MM.

U.S.A.F. FILM LIBRARY CENTER   FREE   SFP 1037

F0133

UNIVERSE

NATIONAL FILM BOARD OF CANADA

A JOURNEY THROUGH SPACE, BEYOND THE SOLAR SYSTEM, INTO
THE FAR REGIONS OF THE SKY NOW PERCEIVED BY ASTRONOMERS.

30 MIN.

F0134   1962   CA

THE 1428 ALPHAMERIC OPTICAL READER

DPD PROMOTIONAL SERVICES
PURCHASE. REGIONAL DPD PROMOTIONAL SERVICE $33.00

THIS FILM VIVIDLY DESCRIBES THE IBM PRINCIPLE OF OPTICAL
CHARACTER READING AND SHOWS DRAMATICALLY THE MANY
OUTSTANDING SALES ADVANTAGES OF THE IBM 1428. THE FILM

F0135   1963   CAB

THE ADA STORY

LOCKHEED MISSILE AND SPACE COMPANY

AN ACCOUNT OF THE AUTOMATION OF CLERICAL EFFORT THROUGH
THE USE OF REMOTELY LOCATED ADA (AUTOMATIC DATA
ACQUISITION) EQUIPMENT CONNECTED DIRECTLY TO A REAL
TIME COMPUTER SYSTEM CONSISTING OF TWO RCA 301 COMPUTERS
AND AN 88 MILLION CHARACTER DATA DISC FILE. THE FILM
DEMONSTRATES THE USE OF THE SYTEM FOR MANUFACTURING
SHOP ORDER STATUS AND LOCATION REPORTING AND PROCUREMENT
INVENTORY CONTROL AT LOCKHEED MISSILE AND SPACE COMPANY.

24 MIN., SD., COLOR, 16 MM.

LOCKHEED SPACE AND MISSILE CO.	FREE	NAME
RCA	FREE	NAME

F0136   1963   C

THE ANALOG COMPUTER AND ITS APPLICATION TO ORDINARY
DIFFERENTIAL EQUATIONS

UNIVERSITY OF MICHIGAN

THIS FILM WAS MADE ESPECIALLY FOR USE IN COURSES ON
ORDINARY DIFFERENTIAL EQUATIONS. IT EXPLAINS THE DESIGN
AND OPERATION OF THE ANALOG COMPUTER AND ILLUSTRATES
ITS VALUE IN THE STUDY OF BOTH LINEAR AND NONLINEAR
EQUATIONS.

30 MIN., SD., B/W, 16 MM.

UNIVERSITY OF MICHIGAN $5.50   NAME

F0137   1963   C B

AUTOMATIC PROCESS CONTROL

INSTRUMENT SOCIETY OF AMERICA
MADE AND RELEASED BY CALVIN PRODUCTIONS

DISCUSSES THE FOUR MODES OF CONTROL-ON/OFF, PROPORTIONAL
WITH RESET, AND PROPORTIONAL WITH RESET AND RATE ACTION,
AND ILLUSTRATES HOW PRODUCT QUALITY AND ECONOMIC RETURN
ARE AFFECTED BY THE ADDITION OF EACH MODE. POINTS OUT THE
RELATIONSHIPS OF SYSTEM ANALYSIS, CENTRALIZED PANELS, AND
COMPUTER CONTROL TO OPTIMUM PROCESS CONDITIONS. SETTING,
A SMALL CHEMICAL PROCESS PLANT.

33 MIN., SD., COLOR, 16 MM.

F0138   1963   SCA

A BETTER WAY. (WITH DATA PROCESSING)

IBM
PURCHASE. HOLLYWOOD ANIMATORS, INC.

SOME UNIQUE APPLICATIONS OF DATA PROCESSING EQUIPMENT.
ABOUT POEPLE WHO HAD A PROBLEM AND FOUND A BETTER WAY
TO SOLVE IT.

30 MIN., SD., COLOR, 16 MM.

IBM   FREE   NAME

F0139   1963   SCA

CANADA-AUTOMATION

CANADA DEPT. OF TRADE AND COMMERCE
MADE AND RELEASED BY NATIONAL FILM BOARD OF CANADA

SHOWS THE MANUFACTURE OF CUSTOM-TAILORED AUTOMATION
EQUIPMENT. FILMED AT THE STANDARD MODERN TOOL PLANT
IN TORONTO.

6 MIN., SD., B/W, 16 MM.

F0140   1963   SCA

COMPUTERS AND HUMAN BEHAVIOR. (FOCUS ON BEHAVIOR SERIES)

> MAYER-SKLAR
> MADE AND RELEASED BY N.E.T. FILM SERVICE
>
> EXPLORES SOME OF THE RESEARCH BEING CONDUCTED AT THE
> CARNEGIE INSTITUTE OF TECHNOLOGY WITH ELECTRONIC DIGITAL
> COMPUTERS IN AN EFFORT TO EVOLVE NEW THEORIES ABOUT HUMAN
> MENTAL PROCESSES. INVESTIGATES PERCEPTION OF MOTION AND
> DEPTH, MEMORIZATION, AND PROBLEM SOLVING. WITH STUDY
> GUIDE.
>
> 30 MIN., SD., B/W, 16 MM.

UNIVERSITY OF CALIFORNIA	$8.00		6446
BRIGHAM YOUNG UNIVERSITY	$4.25	$6.00	NAME
UNIVERSITY OF COLORADO	$4.25	$6.00	NAME
NATIONAL EDUCATIONAL TELEVISION	$5.25		NAME
N.E.T. FILM SERVICE	$5.25		NAME
INDIANA UNIVERSITY	$5.40		ES-712

F0141   1963   JSCA

HOW TO SUCCEED AT CARDS

> IBM
> PURCHASE. TRAINING FILMS, INC.
>
> AN ACCOUNT OF HOW IBM CARDS ARE MANUFACTURED, WITH
> SPECIAL EMPHASIS ON QUALITY CONTROL.
>
> 12 MIN., SD., COLOR, 16 MM.

IBM	FREE	NAME

F0142   1963   CA

IBM 1440-1060 ON-LINE SAVINGS PREMIERE

> IBM
> PURCHASE. TRAINING FILMS, INC.
>
> AN ACTION DESCRIPTION OF THE IBM 1062 PREMIERE SHOWING
> OF THE IBM 1062 ON-LINE TO THE IBM 1440 DATA PROCESSING
> SYSTEM, AS WAS PRESENTED TO FINANCIAL EXECUTIVES FROM
> ACROSS THE COUNTRY WHO WERE INVITED TO ENDICOTT AS
> GUESTS OF IBM. IT TAKES THE VIEWER THROUGH A COLORFUL
> DEMONSTRATION OF THE TELLER TERMINAL, POINTING OUT ITS
> FUNCTIONAL OPERATIONS AND ITS ADVANTAGES TO THE FINANCIAL
> INDUSTRY. SHOWS CLOSE-UPS OF THE IBM 1062 AND 1050
> TERMINALS ON-LINE TO THE 1440 DATA PROCESSING SYSTEM.
>
> 8 MIN., SD., COLOR, 16 MM., 8 MM. FAIRCHILD CARTRIDGE

IBM	FREE	NAME

F0143   1963   CAB

IBM 1710 CONTROL SYSTEM FOR ECONOMIC DISPATCHING IN
UTILITIES

> IBM
> PURCHASE. TRAINING FILMS, INC.
>
> THIS MOVIE WAS MADE IN COOPERATION WITH THE PUBLIC
> SERVICE COMPANY OF NEW MEXICO. IT SHOWS THE DIGITAL
> APPROACH TO THE CONTROL OF ECONOMIC DISPATCH AND
> FREQUENCY OF A POWER SYSTEM. THE STORY OF THIS
> CLOSED-LOOP SYSTEM, INSTALLED IN NINE MONTHS,
> INCLUDES COMMENTS BY THE PRESIDENT AND THE PROJECT
> ENGINEER OF THE PUBLIC SERVICE COMPANY OF NEW MEXICO.
>
> 9 MIN., SD., COLOR, 16 MM.

IBM	FREE	NAME

F0144   1963   CA

IBM 1050 DATA COMMUNICATIONS SYSTEM

> IBM
> PURCHASE. TRAINING FILMS, INC.
>
> THIS FILM ILLUSTRATES THE INCREASING IMPORTANCE OF DATA
> COMMUNICATIONS IN MODERN BUSINESS OPERATIONS. IT PORTRAYS
> THE ABILITY OF THIS SYSTEM TO ECONOMICALLY TRANSMIT DATA
> TO AND FROM ANY LOCATION IN THE COUNTRY, OVER ORDINARY
> COMMUNICATIONS LINES. THE FILM ALSO DEMONSTRATES THE
> SYSTEM'S CAPACITY TO USE ANY COMBINATION OF CARDS, PAPER
> TAPE, EDGE-NUMBERED DOCUMENTS AND HARD COPY.
>
> 12 MIN., SD., COLOR, 16 MM.

IBM	FREE	NAME

F0145   1963   JSCA

INNSBRUCK-TOKYO 1964

> IBM
> PURCHASE. FILM ENTERPRISES, INC.
>
> USING ANIMATION, THIS FILM TRACES THE HISTORY AND
> DEVELOPMENT OF THE OLYMPIC GAMES. WE ARE INTRODUCED
> TO THE 1964 WINTER AND SUMMER GAMES, WITH A DETAILED
> EXPLANATION OF HOW RESULTS OF THE VARIOUS EVENTS WILL
> BE COLLECTED, COMPUTED, AND THEN IMMEDIATELY DISSEMINATED
> AROUND THE WORLD IN RECORD TIME.
>
> 9 MIN., SD., COLOR, 16 MM.

IBM	FREE	NAME

F0146   1963   SCA

INQUIRY

> IBM
> MADE BY HENRY STRAUSS AND COMPANY
> PURCHASE. HENRY STRAUSS PRODUCTIONS
>
> EXPLAINS THE ROLE OF DATA PROCESSING EQUIPMENT IN KEY
> FUNCTIONS OF GOVERNMENT AND SOCIETY. REVIEWS DAY-TO-DAY
> ACTIVITIES OF THE UNITED STATES AIR FORCE, AND SHOWS THE
> ROLE PLAYED BY DATA PROCESSING IN THE SUCCESSFUL
> FULFILLMENT OF THE AIR FORCE'S GLOBAL RESPONSIBILITIES.
>
> 17 MIN., SD., COLOR, 16 MM.

IBM	FREE	NAME
U.S.A.F. FILM LIBRARY CENTER	FREE	SFP 1204

F0147   1963   CA

INTRODUCTION TO ANALOG COMPUTERS

> ARGONNE NATIONAL LABORATORY
> PURCHASE. BYRON, INC. $344.36
>
> THIS TWO-HOUR, THREE-PART TECHNICAL LECTURE-FILM
> (APPROXIMATELY 40 MINUTES PER PART) BY DR. L.C. JUST
> OF ARGONNE'S APPLIED MATHEMATICS DIVISION INCLUDES,
> (1) COMPONENTS OF ELECTRONIC ANALOG COMPUTERS, (2)
> FAMILIARIZATION WITH A TYPICAL ANALOG COMPUTER, (3)
> PROGRAMMING FOR ANALOG COMPUTERS, AND (4) SOLUTION
> OF TYPICAL PROBLEMS.
>
> 120 MIN., SD., COLOR, 16 MM.

ARGONNE NATIONAL LABORATORY	FREE	NAME

F0148   1963   SCA

INVITATION TO THE FUTURE

> IBM WORLD TRADE CORPORATION
> PURCHASE. FILM ACTIVITIES MANAGER, IBM WORLD TRADE CORP.
>
> A CHALLENGING PRESENTATION OF THE CONTINUING DYNAMIC
> EXPANSION OF THE IBM WORLD TRADE CORPORATION. THE FILM
> EMBRACES SOME INTERESTING GLIMPSES OF IBM'S EARLY
> EQUIPMENT AND THEIR MODERN COUNTERPARTS. PROCESS CONTROL,
> NUMERIC CONTROL, INFORMATION RETRIEVAL AND TELE-PROCESSING
> ARE PRESENTED BRIEFLY AS MODERN IBM APPLICATIONS AND
> THEIR POTENTIAL IMPACT ON WORLD MARKETS. WORLD TRADE'S
> NEWEST DEVELOPMENT LABORATORIES AND EDUCATION CENTERS
> ARE ALSO PRESENTED. PRIMARILY AN INTERNAL FILM FOR
> IBM AUDIENCES.
>
> 15 MIN., SD., COLOR, 16 MM.

IBM	FREE	NAME

F0149   1963   SCA

OF MEN AND MACHINES. (FOCUS ON BEHAVIOR SERIES)

> MAYER-SKLAR
> MADE AND RELEASED BY N.E.T. FILM SERVICE
>
> USES THE WORK OF DR. PAUL FITTS OF THE UNIVERSITY OF
> MICHIGAN, DR. JULIAN CHRISTIANSEN OF THE WRIGHT AIR
> DEVELOPMENT CENTER, AND DR. GEORGE BRIGGS OF OHIO STATE
> UNIVERSITY TO INVESTIGATE THE MAN-MACHINE RELATIONSHIP.
> SHOWN ARE SOME OF THE WAYS IN WHICH MAN HANDLES AND
> PROCESSES INFORMATION FEEDBACK BETWEEN MAN AND MACHINES
> AND THE HUMAN BEING'S BEHAVIOR IN HIGHLY COMPLEX MAN-

MACHINE SYSTEMS, WHICH HAS LED TO THE REDESIGN OF
EQUIPMENT. WITH STUDY GUIDE.

30 MIN., SD., B/W, 16 MM.

UNIVERSITY OF CALIFORNIA	$8.00		6445
BRIGHAM YOUNG UNIVERSITY	$4.25	$6.00	NAME
UNIVERSITY OF COLORADO	$4.25	$6.00	NAME
INDIANA UNIVERSITY	$5.40		ES-711

F0150   1963   CAB

A NEW TOOL FOR PROFIT - THE IBM 1440

IBM
PURCHASE. TRAINING FILMS, INC.

THIS MOVIE SETS FORTH THE PLACE OF THE IBM 1440 SYSTEM
IN TODAY'S BUSINESS. IT IS A DEMONSTRATION OF THE SYSTEM,
DESCRIBING THE BASIC FUNDAMENTALS OF INPUT, PROCESSING,
STORAGE AND OUTPUT. IT DRAMATICALLY POINTS UP THE FACT
THAT THE IBM 1440 IS AN IDEAL MANAGEMENT TOOL.

12 MIN., SD., COLOR, 16 MM., 8 MM. FAIRCHILD CARTRIDGE

IBM	FREE	NAME

F0151   1963   CA

PROGRESS REPORT FROM LABORATORIES OF IBM

IBM
PURCHASE. GOTHAM FILM SERVICE

FOUR VIGNETTES SHOW NEW IBM LABORATORY DEVELOPMENTS TO
HELP PROCESS THE ENORMOUS VOLUME OF INFORMATION UTILIZED
BY SCIENCE, BUSINESS, AND GOVERNMENT EVERY DAY. THREE
EXPERIMENTAL SYSTEMS SCAN INFORMATIONAL MATERIAL, PROCESS
IT IN A COMPUTER, STORE AND REPRODUCE IT ON COMMAND.
AUTOMATIC HANDLING OF PRINTED, HANDWRITTEN AND EVEN VISUAL
MATERIALS ARE SEEN. A NEW INJECTION LASER FROM IBM,
SMALLER THAN THE EYE OF A NEEDLE, GENERATES AN INTENSE,
THIN INFORMATION-CARRYING BEAM OF LIGHT FROM ELECTRIC
CURRENT WHICH CAN BE MANIPULATED IN THE MANNER OF RADIO
WAVES FOR MANY DIFFERENT APPLICATIONS.

6 MIN., SD., B/W, 16 MM.

IBM	FREE	NAME

F0152   1963   SCA

PROJECT APOLLO - MANNED FLIGHT TO THE MOON

NASA

THIS FILM SHOWS THE PRINCIPAL STEPS THAT WILL BE TAKEN
BY NASA TO PLACE MEN ON THE MOON AND GET THEM BACK SAFELY
WITHIN THIS DECADE. IT SHOWS THE PRINCIPAL FEATURES OF
THE GEMINI SPACECRAFT, THE MODIFIED TITAN BOOSTER AND THE
TYPE OF OPERATIONS TO BE CARRIED OUT. IT ALSO SHOWS THE
APOLLO SPACECRAFT, THE SATURN 1, 1B, AND 5 BOOSTERS, AND
TYPES OF LAUNCHES TO BE ACCOMPLISHED BY EACH. ALSO SHOWS
THE COMPLETE SEQUENCE OF EVENTS FOR THE MANNED LUNAR
LANDING FROM EARTH LAUNCH TO RETURN.

13 MIN., SD., COLOR, 16 MM.

NASA	FREE	NAME

F0153   1963   CA

QUALITY ASSURANCE NEWS

IBM
PURCHASE. TRAINING FILMS, INC.

ILLUSTRATES THE CONCEPTS OF AN INDUSTRIAL TESTING SYSTEM
AS APPLIED TO QUALITY ASSURANCE TESTING AND FEEDBACK.
THREE EXAMPLES, ALL INSTALLED IN IBM PLANT LOCATIONS,
ARE CITED, COMPONENT TESTING, ASSEMBLY LINE TESTING,
AND ENVIRONMENTAL TESTING. THIS MOVIE IS PARTICULARLY
AIMED AT OPERATING MANAGEMENT, ESPECIALLY IN THE QUALITY
ASSURANCE AREA.

14 MIN., SD., COLOR, 16 MM.

IBM	FREE	NAME

F0154   1963   SCA

THE SCHOOL INFORMATION CENTER

IBM DATA PROCESSING DIVISION
PURCHASE. TRAINING FILMS, INC.

THIS FILM TELLS THE STORY OF HOW DATA PROCESSING
EQUIPMENT IN A SECONDARY SCHOOL SYSTEM CAN MAKE MORE
TIME AVAILABLE FOR PRIME PROCESS OF TEACHING, AND MORE
FACTS AVAILABLE FOR STUDENT COUNSELING. IT IS PRIMARILY
A PRESENTATION OF AUTOMATED STUDENT RECORD ACCOUNTING,
CLASS SCHEDULING, ATTENDANCE RECORDING, GRADE REPORTING,
STUDENT GUIDANCE, PERMANENT STUDENT RECORDS AND CLASS
LIST APPLICATIONS.

12 MIN., SD., COLOR, 16 MM.

IBM	FREE	NAME

F0155   1963   JSCA

SUNDAY LARK

CRESCENDO FILMS
RELEASED BY GEORGE K. ARTHUR-GO PICTURES

PICTURES A SIX-YEAR-OLD GIRL WHO WANDERS INTO NEW YORK'S
WALL STREET ON A SUNDAY AFTERNOON, SHOWING HER INTEREST
IN THE STAPLE GUNS, ELECTRIC PENCIL SHARPENERS, VARIOUS
IBM COMPUTERS, AND OTHER OFFICE PARAPHERNALIA IN A HUGE
EMPTY OFFICE IN A SKYSCRAPER.

11 MIN., SD., B/W, 16 MM.

F0156   1963   C B

U.S.I.AUTOMATION

U.S. INDUSTRIES
MADE BY JOHN D. GOODELL

DEMONSTRATES THE USE OF U.S. INDUSTRIES' AUTOMATION
EQUIPMENT, INCLUDING TRANSFEROBOTS, FEEDER BOWL EQUIPMENT,
AND RELATED MACHINES. INCLUDES VIEWS OF AUTOMATED
MACHINES ASSEMBLING ELECTRICAL FIXTURES, FEEDER BOWLS
PROCESSING A VARIETY OF PARTS, AND AN AUTOMATED CANDY
PACKING MACHINE.

21 MIN., SD., B/W, 16 MM.

F0157   1964   SCA

AREA OF ACTION

IBM WORLD TRADE CORPORATION

THE AWARD-WINNING FILM ON HOW NATIONS IN THE FAR EAST ARE
TURNING TO ELECTRONIC DATA PROCESSING TO INCREASE BUSINESS
EFFICIENCY. THE VIEWER IS INTRODUCED TO THE WOOL INDUSTRY
OF AUSTRALIA, THE BANKING INDUSTRY OF JAPAN. THROUGH
THESE AND OTHER INDUSTRIAL APPLICATIONS IN INDIA, TAIWAN,
AND THAILAND, WE SEE HOW PEOPLE FROM MANY ASIA-PACIFIC
COUNTRIES ARE WORKING TO FURTHER WORLD PEACE THROUGH TRADE.

29 MIN., SD., COLOR, 16 MM.

IBM	FREE	NAME

F0158   1964   CA

BILL OF MATERIAL PROCESSOR-1401-1627 AUTOPLOTTER-1620
DRAFTING SYSTEM

IBM
PURCHASE. ACADEMY FILM PRODUCTION, INC.

THIS FILM IS AN EXCELLENT INTRODUCTION AND BRIEF MACHINE
DEMONSTRATION OF THE THREE APPLICATIONS IN THE TITLE.
ACTUAL MACHINE PREPARATION OF GRAPHIC OUTPUT IS PRESENTED.

17 MIN., SD., COLOR, 16 MM

IBM	FREE	NAME

F0159   1964   CAB

BURROUGHS CORP. NEWSREEL 1964

BURROUGHS CORP.

THIS FILM PRESENTS AN ACTUAL INSTALLATION LOOK AT
BURROUGHS EDP EQUIPMENT IN THE FOLLOWING CATEGORIES,

FINANCE, CHEMICAL AND PETROLEUM, GOVERNMENT, MANUFACTURING, SCIENCE AND MEDICINE, EDUCATION, INTERNATIONAL ADN DEFENSE.

22 MIN., SD., COLOR, 16 MM.

BURROUGHS CORP.   FREE   NAME

F0160   1964   CA

THE COMPUTER AND NUMERICALLY CONTROLLED MACHINE TOOLS

IBM
PURCHASE. TRAINING FILMS, INC.

THIS FILM FULLY DISCUSSES AND ILLUSTRATES THE EASE OF USE AND THE ADVANTAGES OF AD-APT AND AUTOSPOT PROGRAMS FOR NUMERICALLY CONTROLLED MACHINE TOOLS. COMPLETELY COVERED, IN EASY TO FOLLOW ILLUSTRATIONS THAT ARE DIRECTED TOWARD PRODUCTION PERSONNEL ARE ENGLISH-LIKE LANGUAGE STATEMENTS, THE ROLES OF THE MACRO, LOGICAL AND FORTRAN-LIKE STATEMNETS AND THEIR ADVANTAGES. THE 1620-1311 AND 1627 FUNCTIONS ARE DEMONSTRATED. FOR AUTOSPOT THE FOLLOWING FEATURES ARE HIGHLIGHTED, PATTERN MANIPULATION, ROUTINE AUTOMATIC CALCULATIONS, BOLT-HOLE CIRCLE PROGRAMMING AND MATRIX PROGRAMMING, BUTTING TO INPUT VIA PRE-PUNCHED CARDS.

17 MIN., SD., COLOR, 16 MM.

IBM   FREE   NAME

F0161   1964   CA

COMPUTER SKETCHPAD

PRODUCED BY WGBH TV, CAMBRIDGE, MASSACHUSETTS

AN APPLICATION OF THE TX-2 COMPUTER, USING A LIGHT PEN DRAWING LANGUAGE WHICH PERMITS ARBITRARY PICTURE ELEMENTS FROM PREVIOUSLY DEFINED SHAPES. AN EXPANDED VERSION OF EARLIER SKETCHPAD.

30 MIN., SD., B/W, 16 MM.

ELECTRONIC SYSTEMS LABORATORY   FREE   NAME
INDIANA UNIVERSITY $5.40   FS-1130

F0162   1964   CA

THE CONTROL PROGRAM OF IBM OPERATING SYSTEM/360

IBM
PURCHASE. PRECISION FILM LABORATORIES

THIS FILM IS INTENDED TO INFORM AND EDUCATE THE VIEWER ON THE CONCEPTS OF THE CONTROL PROGRAM. IT EXPLAINS THE ADVANTAGES OF AN OPERATING SYSTEM IN TERMS OF THROUGHPUT, TURNAROUND AND USER SERVICES AND ALSO THE RELATIONSHIP WITH OTHER MEMBERS OF THE OPERATING SYSTEM/360 SUCH AS LANGUAGE PROCESSORS, USER PROGRAMS, ETC. DESIGN CHARACTERISTICS FOR ACCOMODATING MODULAR SYSTEM DESIGN AND SYSTEM GROWTH ARE DISCUSSED.

60 MIN., SD., B/W, 16 MM.

IBM   FREE   NAME

F0163   1964   CA

DOCUMENTATION FOR DATA PROCESSING

IBM
PURCHASE. TRAINING FILMS, INC.

A SHORT FILM STRESSING THE IMPORTANCE OF DOCUMENTATION IN THE DATA PROCESSING INSTALLATION. ADDITIONAL EMPHASIS IS PLACED ON IBM ASSISTANCE TO THE USER IN ESTABLISHING GOOD DOCUMENTATION TECHNIQUES.

10 MIN., SD., COLOR, 16 MM.

IBM   FREE   NAME

F0164   1964   JSCA

EGGS TO MARKET. THE STORY OF AUTOMATED EGG PROCESSING

PEGGY KAHANA AND YORAN KAHANA
RELEASED BY FILM ASSOCIATES OF CALIFORNIA

EXPLAINS WHAT HAPPENS TO EGGS IN THE TWENTY-FOUR HOUR PERIOD AFTER FRESH EGGS ARE COLLECTED BY THE FARMER, DESCRIBING THE ROLE OF AUTOMATIC MACHINES AND SKILLED WORKERS. DEMONSTRATES THE HANDLING AND CARE OF CHICKENS ON THE FARM AND THE PREPARATION OF EGGS AT A PROCESSING PLANT WHERE THEY ARE CLEANED, CANDLED, SORTED, WEIGHED, AND PACKAGED FOR MARKET OR SHELLED FOR BAKERY USE. WITH STUDY GUIDE.

11 MIN., SD., COLOR, 16 MM.

F0165   1964   C B

FLIGHT SIMULATION

IBM
PURCHASE. PRECISION FILM LABORATORIES

THE PURPOSE OF THE FILM IS TO INFORM THE AEROSPACE INDUSTRY OF A UNIQUE NEW PROGRAMMING APPROACH TO THE OLD PROBLEM OF REAL-TIME FLIGHT SIMULATION. DEMONSTRATES THE USE OF DIGITAL COMPUTERS IN SOLVING COMPLEX SIMULATION PROBLEMS. THE PROBLEMS OF SAFELY REACHING THE MOON AND BACK ARE DISCUSSED. BEST SUITED FOR THOSE WITH A PARTICULAR INTEREST IN AND KNOWLEDGE OF THE AEROSPACE INDUSTRY.

20 MIN., SD., COLOR, 16 MM.

IBM   FREE   NAME

F0166   1964   CA

THE IBM ADMINISTRATIVE TERMINAL

IBM
PURCHASE. TRAINING FILMS, INC.

DEMONSTRATION OF THE ADMINISTRATIVE TERMINAL SYSTEM ILLUSTRATING EXAMPLES OF ITS CAPABILITIES IN TEXT EDITING AND PROGRAM WRITING. THIS PROGRAM EXTENDS THE CAPABILITY OF THE 1440 OR 1460 TO INCLUDE NEW APPLICATIONS SUCH AS THE PRODUCTION OF MANUALS, BILLS OF MATERIALS, AND PROGRAMS WHILE THE COMPUTER IS PERFORMING TAPE-TO-PRINTER AND CARD-TO-TAPE OPERATIONS.

16 MIN., SD., COLOR, 16 MM.

IBM   FREE   NAME

F0167   1964   CA

IBM 1410/7010 OPERATING SYSTEM

IBM
PURCHASE. TRAINING FILMS, INC.

THIS FILM ILLUSTRATES THE ADVANTAGES INHERENT IN THE 1410/7010 OPERATING SYSTEM. IT EMPHASIZES JOB-TO-JOB PROCESSING AND THE TELE-PROCESSING CAPABILITIES OF THE 1410/7010.

16 MIN., SD., COLOR, 16 MM.

IBM   FREE   NAME

F0168   1964   CA

THE IBM 7740 COMMUNICATION CONTROL SYSTEM

IBM
PURCHASE. TRAINING FILMS, INC.

THIS PRESENTATION DESCRIBES IN DETAIL THE BROAD FUNCTIONAL CAPABILITIES OF THE IBM 7740 COMMUNICATION CONTROL SYSTEM. IDEALLY SUITED FOR SHOWING TO COMMUNICATIONS MANAGERS IN ALL INDUSTRIES.

11 MIN., SD., COLOR, 16 MM.

IBM   FREE   NAME

F0169   1964   CA

IBM SYSTEM/360

IBM
PURCHASE. TRAINING FILMS, INC.

ANNOUNCEMENT OF IBM SYSTEM/360. CONCENTRATES ON IBM DESIGN OBJECTIVES AND THEIR FULFILLMENT IN IBM SYSTEM/360. GENERAL INDUSTRY USES ARE CITED, BUT PRODUCT CAPABILITIES IN THE BROAD SENSE ARE EMPHASIZED.

17 MIN., SD., COLOR, 16 MM.

IBM   FREE   NAME

F0170   1964   CA

IBM SYSTEM/360 CARD PROCESSING POWER

 IBM
 PURCHASE. TRAINING FILMS, INC.

 DESCRIBES THE IBM/360-MODEL 20 CENTRAL PROCESSING UNIT,
THE INPUT-OUTPUT DEVICES AVAILABLE WITH THIS SYSTEM AND
HOW THESE UNITS CAN BE COMBINED TO EFFICIENTLY HANDLE CARD
PROCESSING APPLICATIONS. IT HIGHLIGHTS THE RPG PROGRAM,
WITH EMPHASIS ON THE FACT THAT PERSONS FAMILIAR WITH
CONTROL PANEL WIRING CONCEPT CAN, WITH A MINIMUM OF
TRAINING, USE THE RPG TO WRITE EFFICIENT PROGRAMS.

 10 MIN., SD., COLOR, 16 MM., 8 MM. FAIRCHILD CARTRIDGE

IBM		FREE	NAME

F0171   1964   JSCA

IBM TELE-PROCESSING RIGHT NOW

 IBM
 PURCHASE. TRAINING FILMS, INC.

 AN EXCELLENT REVIEW OF COMMUNICATIONS CONCEPTS WITH TWO
SPECIFIC APPLICATIONS AND THEIR ADVANTAGES COVERED IN
DETAIL. IT POINTS UP THE ENORMOUS POTENTIAL OF
COMMUNICATIONS EQUIPMENT AND ITS IMPACT IN A MEDIUM-SIZED
DRUG COMPANY AND A LARGE MANUFACTURER.

 9 MIN., SD., COLOR, 16 MM.

IBM		FREE	NAME

F0172   1964   CA

IBM 1030 ROAD SHOW

 IBM
 PURCHASE. PRECISION FILM LABORATORIES

 THIS FILM TRACES THE ROUTE THAT THE IBM 1030 ROAD SHOW
TOOK DURING 1963. IT DEMONSTRATES THE IBM 1440 AND 1030
IN A FACTORY CONTROL DEMONSTRATION, AND HIGHLIGHTS THE
FOLLOWING APPLICATIONS, JOB ASSIGNMENT, LABOR REPORT EDIT,
DEPARTMENT WORKLOAD STATUS INQUIRY, WORK AVAILABLE FOR
ASSIGNMENT INQUIRY, EMPLOYEES STATUS INQUIRY (DEPARTMENT,
INDIVIDUAL), MACHINE STATUS BY DEPARTMENT AND INDIVIDUAL,
ORDER PROGRESS.

 12 MIN., SD., B/W, 16 MM.

IBM		FREE	NAME

F0173   1964   CA

THE IBM 2321 DATA CELL DRIVE

 IBM
 PURCHASE. TRAINING FILMS, INC.

 INTRODUCTORY FILM FOR THE IBM 2321 DATA CELL DRIVE. A
QUICK REVIEW OF MODES OF STORAGE AVAILABLE, CONCENTRATING
ON THE 2321 AND NEW APPLICATION AREAS IT SERVES.

 9 MIN., SD., COLOR, 16 MM.

IBM		FREE	NAME

F0174   1964   JSCAB

THE INFORMATION EXPLOSION

 NATIONAL SCIENCE TEACHERS ASSOCIATION
 MADE BY VISION ASSOCIATES

 THE PURPOSE OF THIS INFORMATIVE, BUT NON-TECHNICAL FILM,
IS TO RESTORE BALANCE TO OUR APPRAISAL OF THE COMPUTER'S
TRUE ROLE IN SOCIETY, TO SHOW THAT THE COMPUTER IS THE
TOOL OF MAN RATHER THAN THE REVERSE. THAT MAN DOES THE
THINKING WHICH DIRECTS THE COMPUTER IS CONSTANTLY
EMPHASIZED.

 20 MIN., SD., COLOR, 16 MM.

ASSOCIATION FILMS, INC.	$5.00	NAME

F0175   1964   CA

MASS INFORMATION CONTROL

 RCA

 THE STORY OF RCA'S 3488 MASS RANDOM ACCESS COMPUTER
EQUIPMENT.

 12 MIN., SD., COLOR, 16 MM.

RCA		FREE	NAME

F0176   1964   CA

TIME SHARING

 SYSTEM DEVELOPMENT CORPORATION

 A DESCRIPTION OF THE TIME SHARING PROGRAM SYSTEM
DEVELOPED AT SYSTEM DEVELOPMENT CORPORATION.

 30 MIN., SD., B/W, 16 MM.

 WESTERN ELECTRIC

F0177   1964   SCA

TOMORROW...TODAY

 IBM WORLD TRADE CORPORATION
 MADE BY FILM ENTERPRISES

 A GRAPHIC ILLUSTRATION OF HOW ELECTRONIC DATA PROCESSING
IS SPEEDING ECONOMIC DEVELOPMENT AND EDUCATIONAL PROGRESS
IN LATIN AMERICA. THE FILM DEPICTS THE ADVANCES ALREADY
BEING MADE IN COSTA RICA, PERU, MEXICO, BRAZIL, AND
ARGENTINA.

 28 MIN., SD., COLOR, 16 MM.

IBM		FREE	NAME

F0178   CA

AUTOMATED TEACHING MACHINES

 THE ADVANTAGES OF TEACHING MACHINES ARE SHOWN.
PROGRAMMED LESSON MATERIALS ARE INDICATED TO BE A
NATURAL PART OF AUTOMATED TEACHING DEVICES. THE BASES
OF DETERMINING STUDENT PROGRESS ARE SHOWN TO BE MORE
DISCREET, USING MACHINED PROGRAMMING.

 15 MIN., SD., B/W, 16 MM.

BRIGHAM YOUNG UNIVERSITY	$3.25	$4.50	NAME

F0179   C B

AUTOMATED X-RAY DIFFRACTOMETRY

 BELL TELEPHONE LABORATORIES, INC.

 A METHOD FOR CONDUCTING X-RAY DIFFRACTION STUDIES USING
AN AUTOMATED DIFFRACTOMETER WHOSE OUTPUT IS COMPILED BY
MEANS OF A COMPUTER.

 19 MIN.

F0180   CAB

CHALLENGE FOR TOMORROW

 U.S. INDUSTRIES, INC.

 THE RAPID MARCH OF INDUSTRY TOWARDS AUTOMATION.
DISCUSSES THE EFFECTS ON DISPLACED WORKERS AND THEIR
RETRAINING.

 16 MIN.

F0181   CA

CHALLENGE OF TOMORROW

 RCA

 THIS FILM SHOWS THE SCOPE OF RCA ACTIVITY

 30 MIN.,   COLOR

RCA		FREE	NAME

F0182   CA

A COMPUTER TECHNIQUE FOR PRODUCING ANIMATED MOVIES

BELL TELEPHONE LABORATORIES, INC.

A COMPUTER TECHNIQUE HAS BEEN DEVELOPED FOR THE
PRODUCTION OF ANIMATED DIAGRAM MOVIES AND HAS BEEN
IMPLEMENTED USING AN IBM 7090 COMPUTER AND A STROMBERG-
CARLSON S-C 4020 MICROFILM RECORDER.

17 MIN.

F0183   CAB

THE COMPUTER COMES TO MARKETING

FORTUNE FILMS AND ERNST AND ERNST

MARKETING MEN ARE DISCOVERING THAT COMPUTERS CAN WORK
WONDERS IN HELPING SOLVE MANY OF THE COMPLEX PROBLEMS
OF MARKETING AND DISTRIBUTION. FORTUNE ARTICLES STRESSED
SOME OF THESE NEW MARKETING APPLICATIONS AND FORTUNE HAS
TRANSLATED THE SUBJECT INTO A FILM GIVING AN INSIGHT INTO
MANY COMPUTER APPLICATIONS IN THE WHOLE RANGE OF MARKETING.

30 MIN., SD., B/W, 16 MM.

FORTUNE FILMS   FREE   NAME

F0184   CA

COMPUTING FOR FUN

BELL TELEPHONE LABORATORIES

DR. J.R. PIERCE DESCRIBING HOW COMPUTER MUSIC IS MADE.
EXAMPLES OF THE MUSIC, RANGING FROM SIMPLE TO HIGHLY
COMPLEX ARE PRESENTED.

28 MIN.

F0185   C B

DECISION AT DANSKAMMER

IBM

A FILM REPORT OF HOW AN IBM 1710 CONTROL SYSTEM HELPS
GUIDE OPERATING DECISIONS AT THE DANSKAMMER POINT
GENERATOR STATION OF THE CENTRAL HUDSON CORPORATION.
BEST SUITED TO AUDIENCES WITH A KNOWLEDGE OF INDUSTRIAL
PROCESS CONTROL.

10 MIN., SD., COLOR, 16 MM.

IBM   FREE   NAME

F0186   SCA

DIGITAL COMPUTERS. INTRODUCTION

REMINGTON RAND UNIVAC

REVEALS THE WHAT, HOW, AND WHY OF DIGITAL COMPUTING TODAY.
SO FAST IS THE SPEED OF THESE COMPUTERS INCREASING, THAT
THE FUTURE WILL FIND MACHINES PERFORMING CALCULATIONS IN
NANOSECONDS, WHILE THEIR SIZE WILL BE REDUCED TO THAT OF
A DESK CALCULATOR. FEATURES MAGNETIC DRUMS AND CORES,
RANDOM ACCESS, SOLID STATE, REAL TIME OPERATION, CARD-TO-
TAPE CONVERSION, AND MANY OTHER CHARACTERISTICS.

16 MIN., SD., COLOR, 16 MM.

SYRACUSE UNIVERSITY $6.50   2-4021

F0187   CAB

FUNDAMENTALS OF PERT. FILM SERIES NO. 3

AMERICAN MANAGEMENT ASSOCIATION

IN THIS SERIES, SPEAKERS WILL EXPLAIN THE TECHNIQUES OF
PERT, SUGGESTING THE METHODS IN WHICH PERT CAN HELP YOU
MEASURE THE RELATIVE PROBABILITY OF MEETING PRODUCTION
AND DELIVERY DEADLINES, EXPOSE FUTURE IMPEDIMENTS TO
PROGRESS IN TIME TO PLAN CORRECTIVE ACTION, FORECAST
REPERCUSSIONS OF MINOR AND MAJOR CHANGES IN OPERATION,
ALLOW FUNDS, MANPOWER, OR TIME TO BE USED MORE EFFECTIVELY
IN ACCELERATING PROGRAMS, PERMIT ASSIGNMENT OF RESOURCES

FROM NON-CRITICAL OR AHEAD-OF-SCHEDULE AREAS TO ESSENTIAL
BEHIND-SCHEDULE PRODUCTION AREAS.

SD., B/W, 16 MM.

AMERICAN MANAGEMENT ASSOCIATION $300.00   NAME

F0188   JSCA

IBM AT THE WORLD'S FAIR

IBM

A TOUR THROUGH THE IBM PAVILION AT THE NEW YORK WORLD'S
FAIR, HIGHLIGHTING THE PEOPLE WALL WHICH TAKES VISITORS
ON A TRIP UP INTO THE INFORMATION MACHINE THEATRE. ALSO
SHOWN ARE SEQUENCES FROM SEVERAL PUPPET SHOWS FEATURED
INSIDE THE PAVILION, AS WELL AS THE AUTOMATIC LANGUAGE
TRANSLATION AND CHARACTER RECOGNITION EXHIBITS.

6 MIN., SD., COLOR, 16 MM.

IBM   FREE   NAME

F0189   CAB

INTEGRATED DATA PROCESSING

NATIONAL OFFICE MANAGEMENT ASSOCIATION

NOMA HAS BROUGHT TOGETHER A FILM PRESENTING THE MACHINES
AND EQUIPMENT PRODUCED BY 14 OF THE NATION'S MAJOR
MANUFACTURERS. A COMPREHENSIVE, NON-COMMERCIAL FILM
STORY DEPICTING THE WAYS IN WHICH VARIOUS PIECES OF IDP
EQUIPMENT MAY BE INCORPORATED INTO AN EFFICIENT, MODERN
DATA PROCESSING SYSTEM. SHOWS HOW THE VARIOUS MACHINES
ACTUALLY HANDLE PURCHASING, SALES ORDER INVENTORY CONTROL,
SHIPPING RECORDS, PRODUCTION PLANNING, ACCOUNTS PAYABLE
AND RECEIVABLE, AND STATISTICAL INFORMATION.

35 MIN., SD., COLOR, 16 MM.

BUSINESS EDUCATION FILMS $20.00   NAME

F0190   1964   CAB

JOSS

RAND CORPORATION

A DETAILED PRESENTATION OF RAND'S SYSTEM FOR ACCESS TO
A COMPUTER THROUGH REMOTE CONTROL TYPEWRITER STATIONS.
ILLUSTRATIONS INCLUDE HOW PROGRAMS MAY BE WRITTEN, REVISED,
RUN, EXPERIMENTED WITH AND PRINTED FOR FURTHER USE, ALL
WITHOUT THE USER LEAVING HIS OFFICE.

23 MIN.

RAND CORPORATION   FREE   NAME

F0191   CA

LOGIC ON A CHIP

RADIO CORPORATION OF AMERICA

THIS FILM SHOWS MONOLITHIC INTEGRATED CIRCUITRY.

COLOR

RCA   FREE   NAME

F0192   CA

MAGNETIC TAPES

IBM

AN ACCOUNT OF HOW IBM TESTS MAGNETIC TAPE PRODUCTS BEFORE
RELEASING THEM FOR SHIPMENT TO CUSTOMERS. RELATES RIGID
SPECIFICATIONS TO THE NEED FOR QUALITY TAPE IN A DATA
PROCESSING INSTALLATION. BEST SUITED FOR ADULT GROUPS
WITH SOME INTEREST IN MAGNETIC TAPE USE OR DATA PROCESSING.

12 MIN., SD., COLOR, 16 MM.

IBM   FREE   NAME

F0193   SCA

MARK OF MAN

GENERAL DYNAMICS CORPORATION

TRACES HISTORY OF MAN'S EFFORTS TO RECORD INFORMATION
FROM THE MARKS MADE ON WALLS OF 'CAVES, THROUGH THE
DEVELOPMENT OF MECHANICAL PRINTING DEVICES TO HIGH-SPEED
RECORDING OF COMPUTER DATA BY CATHODE RAY TUBE.

10 MIN., SD., COLOR, 16 MM.

ELECTRONIC DIVISION OF GENERAL DYNAMICS CORPORATION

F0194   CA

NCR 420-1 OPTICAL CHARACTER SCANNER

NATIONAL CASH REGISTER COMPANY

THIS FILM DESCRIBES HOW THE SCANNER READS OPTICAL FONT
CHARACTERS, HOW IT USES ITS OWN LOGIC TO EITHER ACCEPT
OR REJECT THE CHARACTER AND HOW IT OUTPUTS EDITED
INFORMATION TO A DATA PROCESSING SYSTEM AND HOW OPTICAL
SCANNING FITS INTO SUCH A SYSTEM.

20 MIN., SD., COLOR, 16 MM.

NATIONAL CASH REGISTER COMPANY

F0195   SCA

ONCE UPON A PUNCHED CARD

IBM

AN EASY-TO-UNDERSTAND EXPLANATION OF THE BASIC PRINCIPLES
OF PUNCHED CARD ACCOUNTING. DEMONSTRATES HOW TO DO A
ROUTINE ACCOUNTING JOB MORE EFFICIENTLY AND ECONOMICALLY,
COMPARED TO MANUAL METHODS, AND AT THE SAME TIME IMPROVE
BUSINESS CONTROL.

9 MIN., SD., COLOR, 16 MM.

IBM   FREE   NAME

F0196   CAB

OPERATING SYSTEMS. WHY AND HOW

IBM

A LECTURE BY MR. BERNARD WITT DISCUSSING THE REASONS FOR
HAVING AN OPERATING SYSTEM AND HOW IBM HAS CHOSEN TO
IMPLEMENT AN OPERATING SYSTEM.

60 MIN.

F0197   CAB

PERT APPLICATIONS AND PRINCIPLES

AMERICAN MANAGEMENT ASSOCIATION

BEGINNING WITH A BRIEF HISTORY OF THE PROGRAM EVALUATION
AND REVIEW TECHNIQUE, MR. CODIER THEN GOES ON TO DESCRIBE
WHAT PERT IS AND WHAT YOU CAN HOPE TO ACCOMPLISH BY USING
IT. FURTHER, HE CONSIDERS THE UNDERLYING PHILOSOPHY WHICH
HE FEELS WILL MAKE OR BREAK THE SUCCESS OF THE APPLICATION
OF ANY MANAGEMENT SYSTEM. HE BREAKS PERT DOWN TO ITS
SIMPLEST TERMS, USING HYPOTHETICAL CASES TO EXPLAIN ITS
OPERATION, EFFECTIVENESS AND ADVANTAGES OVER MORE
PRIMITIVE METHODS. HE ALSO EXPLAINS THE FOUR PERT RULES
WHICH HE CONSIDERS OF FUNDAMENTAL IMPORTANCE.

39 MIN., SD., B/W, 16 MM.

AMERICAN MANAGEMENT ASSOCIATION $60.00   6-1

F0198   SCA

PILOT FOR ATLAS

THE BURROUGHS CORPORATION

A SHORT PRESENTATION ON THE COMPUTER REQUIREMENTS FOR THE
ATLAS MISSILE FLIGHTS.

6 MIN.

F0199   CA

PLOTLINES

ELECTRONIC ASSOCIATES, INC.

DESCRIBES THE SIGNIFICANCE OF DATAPLOTTER ANALYSIS OF
DATA PROCESSING INFORMATION. INCLUDED ARE APPLICATIONS
MAKING WEATHER MAPS, OIL EXPLORATION MAPS AND U.S.
GOVERNMENT MARKET SHEETS.

22 MIN., SD.,   16 MM.

ELECTRONIC ASSOCIATES, INC.

F0200   CAB

PRINCIPLES OF RELIABILITY

THE MARTIN COMPANY SPACE SYSTEMS DIVISION

AN ANIMATED, HUMOROUS TREATMENT OF THE CONCEPT OF
RELIABILITY RELATIVE TO REQUIREMENTS FOR COMPLEX EQUIPMENT.

13 MIN.

F0201   CAB

PROFITABLE COMPUTER SYSTEMS

AMERICAN MANAGEMENT ASSOCIATION

MR. FIELD EXAMINES A WIDE SPHERE OF MANAGEMENT ACTIVITIES,
PREDICTING THAT IN THE NEXT DECADE, BUSINESS SYSTEMS
ENGINEERING AND THE COMPUTER SHOULD PROVIDE THE MAJOR
GROWTH IN NATIONAL PRODUCTIVITY. HE EXPLAINS HOW COMPUTER
SYSTEMS HAVE HELPED COMPANIES EXPAND, CUT COSTS, IMPROVE
OPERATIONS, BOOST PROFITS. HE ALSO DEMONSTRATES HOW
EXECUTIVES CAN INCREASE THEIR EFFICIENCY AND EFFECTIVENESS
BY UTILIZING THE VAST RESOURCES OF THIS INCREASINGLY
IMPORTANT MANAGEMENT TOOL.

40 MIN., SD., B/W, 16 MM.

AMERICAN MANAGEMENT ASSOCIATION $60.00   6-2

F0202   CA

PROGRAMMING LANGUAGES

SYSTEM DEVELOPMENT CORPORATION

DESIGNED AS AN INTRODUCTION TO PROGRAMMING LANGUAGES
IN COMPUTER-ORIENTED SYSTEMS, AND TOUCHING UPON THE
EVOLUTION OF THE SDC COMPILER LANGUAGE CALLED JOVIAL,
THIS FILM IS A PLEASANT AID FOR LIVE BRIEFING SESSIONS
ON THE WHY OF ALL SUCH LANGUAGES. IT CAN BE USEFUL AS
A POINT OF DEPARTURE FOR DISCUSSIONS OR IN ORIENTING
BEGINNERS TO PROGRAMMING PROBLEMS. IT ILLUSTRATES ONE
OF MANY SIMPLE WAYS OF INTRODUCING NON-PROGRAMMERS
TO PROGRAMMING.

5 MIN., SD., COLOR, 16 MM.

SYSTEM DEVELOPMENT CORPORATION   FREE   F-23

F0203   CAB

PROGRESS IN NUMERICAL CONTROL

BENDIX CORPORATION, INDUSTRIAL CONTROL DIVISION

DESCRIBES APPLICATIONS OF NUMERICAL CONTROL SYSTEMS
USING THE DYNAPATH 20. APPLICATIONS INCLUDE MACHINE
TOOL CONFIGURATIONS, TOOL CHANGING AND PROFILE MILLING
MACHINES.

22 MIN.

F0204   JSCA

PUSHBUTTONS AND PROBLEMS

HEARST METROTONE NEWS

TRACES THE DEVELOPMENT OF AUTOMATION, BEGINNING WITH
HENRY FORD'S ASSEMBLY LINE. DESCRIBES ITS SPREAD TO
OTHER INDUSTRIES, WHICH RESULTS IN HIGHER WAGES, A
SHORTER WORK WEEK, AND MORE LEISURE. DESCRIBES THE
PROBLEMS THAT HAVE ARISEN AS AUTOMATION INCREASES AND
SPREADS TO AGRICULTURE, TELEPHONE COMMUNICATIONS, AND
MASS PRODUCTION IN SUCH AREAS AS DRUGS AND PRESCRIPTIONS.

EMPHASIZES THE ROLE OF MANAGEMENT AND LABOR IN SOLVING
THE UNEMPLOYMENT PROBLEM.

10 MIN., SD., B/W, 16 MM.

BRIGHAM YOUNG UNIVERSITY	$2.25	$3.25	NAME
UNIVERSITY OF COLORADO	$2.25	$6.00	NAME

F0205   CAB

PUSH BUTTON TAXES

UNITED STATES INTERNAL REVENUE SERVICE

COMPUTER USAGE IN A LARGE-SCALE TASK OF FEDERAL INCOME
TAX ADMINISTRATION, AND INTRODUCTORY OVERVIEW OF THE
SEVERAL STEPS, PROCESSES, SAVINGS, AND EQUITY OF ACCURATE
ACCOUNTING.

10 MIN.

F0206   CA

RCA MASS RANDOM ACCESS MEMORY EQUIPMENT 3488

RCA

A FILM ON THE APPLICATIONS OF 5 BILLION CHARACTER
CAPACITY MAGNETIC CARD MEMORY SYSTEM.

8 MIN., SD., COLOR,

RCA	FREE	NAME

F0207   CAB

REAL TIME TELETYPE

GENERAL ELECTRIC COMPANY AND CHRYSLER CORPORATION

DESCRIBES THE USE BY CHRYSLER CORPORATION OF A GE DATANET
30 SYSTEM AS A COMMUNICATIONS PROCESSOR IN THEIR WORLD-
WIDE DATA COMMUNICATION, SERVING AS A MESSAGE SWITCHING
CENTER, REPLACING A TORN TAPE SYSTEM.

19 MIN.

F0208   JSCA

TO HARE IS HUMAN

UNIVAC

BUGS BUNNY FIGHTS FOR HIS LIFE AGAINST THE COYOTE AND
HIS COMPUTER.

8 MIN., SD., COLOR, 16 MM.

UNIVAC DIV., SPERRY RAND CORP.	FREE	NAME

F0209   1964   JSCA

TOMORROW'S PROGRAMMERS

RAND CORP.

A NEW FILM THAT IS A FILM RECORD OF A SUMMER CLASS IN
COMPUTING. THE STUDENTS WERE BRIGHT TWELVE YEAR OLDS.

25 MIN.

RAND CORPORATION	FREE	NAME

F0210   SCA

VALLEY TOWN

PRESENTS A DOCUMENTARY STUDY OF AN IMPORTANT FACTOR IN
THE UNEMPLOYMENT PROBLEM, THAT OF WORKERS DISPLACED BY
AUTOMATIC MACHINERY. VALLEY TOWN IS A TYPICAL AMIERICAN
STEEL TOWN IN THE NINETEEN-TWENTIES AND THIRTIES.
EXPLAINS HOW THE WAR MADE SUCH A DEMAND ON THE MAN POWER
THAT THERE WAS A SCARCITY OF MEN ADEQUATELY TRAINED FOR
THE JOB, AND THAT THIS COUNTRY MUST IN THE FUTURE ASSURE
THE TRAINING OF SKILLED WORKERS.

27 MIN., SD., B/W, 16 MM.

UNIVERSITY OF NEVADA	$4.25	$6.00	NAME

F0211   CA

WORLD ORBIT DISPLAY

STROMBERG-CARLSON CORPORATION

COMPUTER GENERATED MOVIES PRODUCED USING THE SC 4020.
A RECTANGULAR BOX ORBITING THE EARTH IS VIEWED FROM
DIFFERENT REFERENCE PLANES.

5 MIN.

F0212   1965   CA

THE IBM INSURANCE INFORMATION SYSTEM

IBM
PURCHASE. TRAINING FILMS, INC.

A SUCCINCT PRESENTATION OF WHAT AN INFORMATION SYSTEM IS,
WHAT IT DOES AND THE IBM EQUIPMENT REQUIRED TO MAKE IT,
FUNCTION.

10 MIN., SD., COLOR, 16 MM.

IBM	FREE	NAME

F0213   1965   CA

**THE IBM 2260 DISPLAY STATION...VITAL LINK IN THE TELEPHONE
SYSTEM**

IBM
PURCHASE. TRAINING FILMS, INC.

THIS FILM FEATURES THE IBM 2260 VISUAL DISPLAY STATION
IN A DEMONSTRATION OF VARIOUS TECHNIQUES SUCH AS DATA
INPUT, DATA CORRECTION, INQUIRY AND OTHER APPLICATIONS
AS USED BY A TELEPHONE COMPANY SERVICE REPRESENTATIVE.

20 MIN., SD., COLOR, 16 MM.

IBM	FREE	NAME

F0214   1965   CAB

QUALITY FOR PROFIT...WITH IBM INDUSTRIAL TESTING SYSTEMS

IBM
PURCHASE. TRAINING FILMS, INC.

A FILMED DEMONSTRATION OF TRANSMISSION TESTING AT FORD-
MORRISTOWN, BEARING TESTING AT SKF-PHILADELPHIA, AND
DISK TESTING AT IBM-SAN JOSE, USING IBM 1710 INDUSTRIAL
TESTING SYSTEM. SUITABLE FOR PROSPECT AND CUSTOMER
VIEWING.

15 MIN., SD., COLOR, 16 MM.

IBM	FREE	NAME

F0215   1960   CA

LOGISTIC SUPPORT MANAGEMENT FOR ADVANCED WEAPONS

U.S. AIR FORCE

EXPLAINS THE MISSION OF A BALLISTIC MISSILE SQUADRON
AND COMPONENTS WHICH MAKE UP THE WEAPON SYSTEMS. SHOWS
HOW LOGISTIC SUPPORT MANAGEMENT PROVIDES PROMPT AND
ACCURATE DATA AND THE VITAL PART PLAYED BY ELECTRONIC
DATA PROCESSING CENTER. EXPLAINS PROCEDURES IN MANAGEMENT
BY EXCEPTION.

20 MIN., SD., COLOR, 16 MM.

U.S.A.F. FILM LIBRARY CENTER	FREE	SFP 669

F0216   1961   CA

THE HANSCOM COMPLEX

U.S. AIR FORCE

PORTRAYS THE MISSION AND SCOPE OF THE HANSCOM COMPLEX,
THE ELECTRONICS RESEARCH AND DEVELOPMENT CENTER AT HANSCOM
FIELD, MASSACHUSETTS. HERE ELECTRONIC SYSTEMS FOR COMMAND
AND CONTROL OF AEROSPACE FORCES AND VEHICLES ARE DESIGNED
AND DEVELOPED.

14 MIN., SD., B/W, 16 MM.

U.S.A.F. FILM LIBRARY CENTER	FREE	SFP 1061

F0217   1963   C B

  U.S. AIR FORCE

PROGRAMMED LEARNING IN THE UNITED STATES AIR FORCE

  DESCRIBES PRINCIPLES OF PROGRAMMED LEARNING, AND EXPLAINS
HOW THE AIR FORCE IS USING THIS REVOLUTIONARY TEACHING
METHOD TO INCREASE QUALITY AND QUANTITY OF AIR FORCE
INSTRUCTION WITH A DECREASE IN TRAINING COST. DEFINES
AND ILLUSTRATES THREE PRINCIPAL TYPES OF PROGRAMMING,
LINEAR, BRANCHING, AND MATHEMATICS. EXPLAINS THEIR
ADVANTAGES OVER TRADITIONAL TRAINING METHODS. PICTURES
THE SYSTEM IN OPERATION AT RANDLOPH AND LACKLAND AIR
FORCE BASES, AIR UNIVERSITY, AND AIR FORCE ACADEMY.

  26 MIN., SD., COLOR, 16 MM.

  U.S.A.F. FILM CENTER   FREE   TF 5525

F0218   1961   CAB

THE SECONDARY SCHOOL AND COMPUTERS

  RAND CORPORATION

  FRED GRUENBERGER ADDRESSES A MESSAGE TO SECONDARY SCHOOL
MATHEMATICS TEACHERS. USING AN IBM 1620 COMPUTER IN
ACTION, HE SHOWS SOME OF THE THINGS WHICH A COMPUTER CAN
DO IN A HIGH SCHOOL. DEMONSTRATES HOW TO SOLVE FOUR
SIMULTANEOUS LINEAR EQUATIONS, DIOPHANTINE EQUATIONS, AND
PRIME NUMBERS GENERATION ON A COMPUTER.

  20 MIN., SD., B/W, 16 MM.

  RAND CORPORATION   FREE   NAME

F0219   CAB

NCR 315 DATA PROCESSING SYSTEM FEATURING CRAM

  NATIONAL CASH REGISTER COMPANY

  25 MIN., SD., COLOR, 16 MM.

  NATIONAL CASH REGISTER COMPANY

F0220   CAB

THE ON-LINE STORY

  NATIONAL CASH REGISTER COMPANY

  34 MIN., SD., COLOR, 16 MM.

  NATIONAL CASH REGISTER COMPANY   FREE   NAME

F0221   1959   CA

APT

  WGBH TV, CAMBRIDGE, MASSACHUSETTS

  FILM OF AN EDUCATIONAL TV PROGRAM DESCRIBING THE
AUTOMATICALLY PROGRAMMED TOOL OR APT SYSTEM. THE
PROGRAM DESCRIBES THE PREPARATION OF CONTROL TAPES
FOR NUMERICALLY CONTROLLED MACHINE TOOLS THROUGH THE
USE OF THE ENGLISH-LIKE APT LANGUAGE FOR PART PROGRAMMING.
THE LANGUAGE IS TRANSLATED AND EXECUTED BY THE APT
SYSTEM OF PROGRAMS, WHICH TRANSFORM A GENERAL-PURPOSE
COMPUTER INTO THE SPECIALIZED APT COMPUTER.

       SD., B/W, 16 MM.

  ELECTRONIC SYSTEMS LABORATORY   FREE   NAME

F0222   1965   C B

COMPUTER ASSISTED INSTRUCTION IN CUSTOMER ENGINEERING

  IBM

  DESCRIBES HOW COMPUTER ASSISTED INSTRUCTION MIGHT POSSIBLE
BE USED IN THE FIELD ENGINEERING DIVISION AFTER IT PROVES
FEASIBLE. COVERS INFORMATION RETRIEVAL, EDUCATION
SIMULATION, FLOATING SUMMARIZATION, USE OF DISPLAYS WITH
COMPUTER ASSISTED INSTRUCTION, AND THE GENERAL CONCEPT OF
REMOTE EDUCATION VIA COMPUTER ASSISTED INSTRUCTION.
DESCRIBES AN EXPLORATORY COMPUTER ASSISTED INSTRUCTIONAL
USE.

  11 MIN., SD., COLOR, 16 MM.

  IBM   FREE   NAME

F0223   1964   SCA

DESTINATION DOWN RANGE

  IBM

  IBM'S ADVANCED DIGITAL COMPUTER HAS BEEN INTEGRATED AND
TESTED WITH AC SPARK PLUG'S INERTIAL MEASURING UNIT.
RESULT. ACHIEVER, THE GUIDANCE SYSTEM FOR TITAN II ICBM.
INCLUDES ASSEMBLY, INTEGRATION, SLED TESTING AND LAUNCH.

  11 MIN., SD., COLOR, 16 MM.

  IBM   FREE   NAME

F0224   1965   C B

EXECUTIVE MICRO-PROCESSING

  IBM

  SHOWS ADVANTAGES OF IBM MICRO PROCESSING SYSTEMS FOR
ENGINEERING DRAWING APPLICATIONS.

  14 MIN., SD., COLOR, 16 MM. AND 8 MM. FAIRCHILD CARTRIDGE

  IBM   FREE   NAME

F0225   1965   JSCA

GEMINI GT-2

  IBM

  NEWSFILM ON UNMANNED GT-2 FLIGHT IN JANUARY.

  10 MIN., SD., COLOR, 16 MM.

  IBM   FREE   NAME

F0226   1965   PJSCA

IBM WORLD'S FAIR PUPPET SHOWS

  IBM
  PURCHASE. CHARLES EAMES PRODUCTIONS

  PRESENTS TWO OF THE PUPPET SHOWS AT IBM'S NEW YORK WORLD'S
FAIR PALILION. IN ONE, SHERLOCK HOLMES SOLVES A MYSTERY
USING COMPUTER LOGIC. IN THE OTHER, A TOWN CELEBRATES THE
INSTALLATION OF ITS FIRST COMPUTER.

  10 MIN., SD., COLOR, 16 MM.

  IBM   FREE   NAME

F0227   1965   SCA

PACEMAKERS

  IBM WORLD TRADE
  PURCHASE. MR. J.G. DAMON, WORLD TRADE HEADQUARTERS

  HOW SEVERAL COUNTRIES IN LATIN AMERICA ARE BENEFITING FROM
ELECTRONIC DATA PROCESSING IN GOVERNMENT AND BUSINESS
APPLICATIONS -- A HOUSING INDUSTRY IN JAMAICA, A TEXTILE
INDUSTRY IN COLOMBIA STEEL PRODUCTION IN CHILE AND
VENEZUELA, AND SOCIAL SECURITY IN CHILE.

  18 MIN., SD., COLOR, 16 MM.

  IBM   FREE   NAME

F0228   1965   CA

PROFILES

  IBM WORLD TRADE
  PURCHASE. MR. J.G. DAMON, WORLD TRADE HEADQUARTERS

  STORY OF GOVERNMENT APPLICATIONS AT WORK IN SEVERAL
COUNTRIES COMPRISING THE ASIA-PACIFIC AREA IN TERMS OF
BENEFITS TO PEOPLE. UNUSUAL AND PROGRESSIVE GOVERNMENT
PROGRAMS THAT UTILIZE IBM SERVICES ARE GRAPHICALLY SHOWN...
NEW ZEALAND'S SOCIAL SECURITY PROGRAM, A GOVERNMENT CLASS
AT THE IBM EDUCATION CENTER IN KUALA LAMPUR, THE
PHILLIPINE AIR FORCE CONDUCTING AERIAL MAPPING OF THE
COUNTRY, AND NHK, THE VAST GOVERNMENT TELEVISION NETWORK
IN JAPAN.

  25 MIN., SD., COLOR, 16 MM.

  IBM   FREE   NAME

F0229   C B

CONTROL BY ANALOGUE

EXECUTIVE FILMS FOR ELECTRONIC ASSOCIATES, INC.

THIS BRITISH FILM DEMONSTRATES ON-LINE ANALOG PROGRAM CONTROL OF INDUSTRIAL PROCESSES, FOR BOTH RESEARCH AND PRODUCTION. COMPUTER SIMULATION IS USED FOR THE DETERMINATION OF OPTIMUM CONDITIONS.

11 MIN., SD., COLOR

F0230   1965   A B

ADVANCED APOLLO LUNAR LANDING SIMULATOR

NAA, S AND ID

SIMULATED LANDINGS ON THE MOON SURFACE ARE SHOWN USING THE ADVANCED APOLLO LUNAR LANDING SIMULATOR DEVELOPED AT NORTH AMERICAN AVIATION, INC.

15 MIN., SD., COLOR

F0231   C B

DESIGN AUGMENTED BY COMPUTERS

GENERAL MOTORS RESEARCH LAB

A NEW AUTOMOBILE IS DESIGNED WITH THE AID OF A TIME-SHARED COMPUTER. MAN-COMPUTER GRAPHIC COMMUNICATION USING A CONSOLE DESIGNED BY GENERAL MOTORS RESEARCH IS DEPICTED. THE ENGINEERING DESIGNER USES A LIGHT PEN TO MODIFY A DESIGN DISPLAYED ON THE GRAPHIC CONSOLE CRT.

13 MIN., SD., COLOR,

F0232   SCAB

THESEUS

BELL LABS

A MECHANICAL MOUSE LEARNS HIS WAY THROUGH A MAZE.

8 MIN., SD., B/W

F0233   1965   SCAB

EVOLUTION OF PROGRAMMING

IMPOSSIBLE BUDGET MOVIES

THIS DELIGHTFUL, HILARIOUS FILM, CONCOCTED FOR THE MARCH, 1965, MEETING OF SHARE, IS A MASTERPIECE OF SATIRE. STARTING WITH THE CAVEMAN PROGRAMMER, IT DEPICTS HUMOROUSLY THE PROGRESS (+) MADE IN PROGRAMMING.

7 MIN., SD., B/W

F0234   1965   CAB

ONE STEP BEHIND - ONE STEP AHEAD

STATE OF NEW YORK AND SYSTEM DEVELOPMENT CORP.

AN OPERATIONAL DESCRIPTION OF HOW THE COMPUTER-BASED NEW YORK STATE IDENTIFICATION AND INTELLIGENCE SYSTEM WILL SERVE THE FUNCTIONS OF POLICE, PROSECUTION, COURTS, PROBATION, CORRECTION AND PAROLE AGENCIES. THE INTERRELATIONSHIPS OF THESE AGENCIES WITH A CENTRAL COMPUTER IS ILLUSTRATED AROUND A DRAMATIC FRAMEWORK.

28 MIN., SD., B/W

F0235

SPACE COMMUNICATIONS

UNITED STATES AIR FORCE

HIGHLIGHTS BASIC PRINCIPLES AND TECHNIQUES OF COMMUNICATIONS, STRESSING THOSE FACTORS THAT RELATE DIRECTLY TO SPACE. EXPLAINS BEHAVIOR OF ELECTROMAGNETIC WAVES AND FORMULA FOR COMPUTING THEIR ATTENUATION RATE. DISCUSSES FACTORS SUCH AS DISTANCE, PAYLOADS, POWER SUPPLY LONGEVITY, MOTION ENVIRONMENT, AND MODES OF TRANSMISSION WITH EMPHASIS ON TELEMETRY.

19 MIN.

F0236

HOW TO SUCCEED WITHOUT REINVENTING THE WHEEL

ODDR AND E

DESCRIBES HOW AN INFORMATION RETRIEVAL SYSTEM IS OF BENEFIT TO AN ENGINEER.

30 MIN.

F0237

XVIII OLYMPIC GAMES - TOKYO

IBM

THIS FILM CONCERNS ITSELF WITH HOW DATA PROCESSING WAS INVOLVED IN THE SCORING AND RESULTS-HANDLING AT THE TOKYO OLYMPICS.

19 MIN.

IBM   FREE

F0238

KARTRAK

SYLVANIA

DESCRIPTION OF THE APPLICATION OF AN AUTOMATIC RAILROAD CAR IDENTIFICATION SYSTEM IN CAR CONTROL.

9 MIN.

F0239

CHILD OF THE FUTURE

NATIONAL FILM BOARD OF CANADA

THE FILM EXAMINES SOME OF THE WAYS IN WHICH TECHNOLOGY IS BEING USED IN THE CLASSROOM. IT SHOWS HOW SCHOOLS AND COLLEGES ARE SHEDDING THEIR TRADITIONAL APATHY TO MACHINES AND ARE NOW EXPLOITING ALL MANNER OF MECHANICAL AND ELECTRONIC AIDS.

59 MIN.

F0240   1965

MACHINES THAT THINK

ARGONNE NATIONAL LABORATORY

RESEARCH AT ARGONNE INTO THE FUTURE SCIENTIFIC USES OF ELECTRONIC COMPUTERS IS SHOWN IN THIS PRESENTATION THAT STRESSES NONNUMERICAL MANIPULATIONS OF SYMBOLS. COMPUTERS ARE TAUGHT TO MAKE QUALITATIVE JUDGMENTS, TO INTERPRET THE SIGNIFICANCE OF PATTERNS SUCH AS SPARK CHAMBER PHOTOGRAPHS, AND TO CONTROL LABORATORY EXPERIMENTAL APPARATUS.

29 MIN., SD., B/W

AEC HEADQUARTERS FILM LIBRARY   FREE   NAME

F0241   SCA

PROFILE OF A HIGHWAY

NET

EXPLAINS THE USE OF DATA-PROCESSING TECHNIQUES WHICH PRECEDE TODAY'S ROAD-BUILDING OPERATIONS AND DEMONSTRATES THE GATHERING OF TERRAIN DATA FROM AERIAL PHOTOGRAPHS FROM WHICH HIGHWAY COST ESTIMATES ARE MADE. SHOWS A COMPUTER SYSTEM WHICH AUTOMATICALLY PRODUCES BLUEPRINT DRAWINGS FROM COLLECTED DATA. POINTS OUT THAT SUCH TECHNIQUES ALLOW ENGINEERS TO INCREASE TRANSPORTAION EFFICIENCY WITH A MINIMUM OF COST.

30 MIN., SD., B/W, 16 MM.

INDIANA UNIVERSITY $5.40   IS-598

F0242

AUTOMATION - THE NEXT REVOLUTION

MCGRAW-HILL $150.00

ADAPTED FROM THE ORIGINAL CBS NEWS PRODUCTION, THIS TIMELY FILM PINPOINTS THE SERIOUS SOCIAL AND ECONOMIC

PROBLEMS OF AUTOMATION, AND THE NEED FOR MASSIVE EFFORT TO
CREATE JOBS AND OVERCOME THESE PROBLEM. THROUGHOUT THE
FILM, WORKERS, LABOR LEADERS, AND INDUSTRIALISTS DISCUSS
TODAY'S ECONOMIC PROGRESS. YOUR STUDENTS SEE AUTOMATION
REVEALED AS THE DOMINANT FACTOR IN THE NEW INDUSTRIAL
REVOLUTION.

28 MIN., SD., B/W, 16 MM.

F0243   1966   CA

PROGRAMMING IN FORTRAN IV

    UNIVERSITY OF CALIFORNIA
    PURCHASE. THE ASSOCIATED STUDENT BOOK STORE

    A COMPUTER PROGRAMMING COURSE CONSISTING OF 14 LECTURES.
THE OBJECTIVE OF THE COURSE IS TO TEACH STUDENTS HOW TO

PROGRAM USING THE FORTRAN LANGUAGE.
PARTIAL CONTENTS ARE AS FOLLOWS.
1. INTRODUCTION TO COMPUTERS
2. ELEMENTS OF THE FORTRAN LANGUAGE
3. WRITING A FORTRAN PROGRAM
4. EXTENDING INPUT-OUTPUT CAPABILITIES
5. FLOW CHARTING, SYMBOLS AND APPLICATION
6. MANIPULATING ALPHABETIC INFORMATION
7. LOOPING PROCEDURES
8. SUBSCRIPTED VARIABLES, ONE DIMENSIONAL ARRAYS
9. HIGHER DIMENSIONAL ARRAYS
10. FUNCTIONS
11. SUBPROGRAMS, SUBROUTINE
12. SUBPROGRAMS, EXTERNAL
13. LOGICAL VARIABLES AND FUNCTIONS
14. SEGMENTING PROGRAMS. SUMMARY

30 MIN. EACH, SD., B/W, 16 MM. (KINESCOPE)

UNIVERSITY OF CALIFORNIA $10.00 EACH   NAME

DIRECTORY OF FILM DEPOSITORIES

ACADEMY FILM PRODUCTION, INC.
123 WEST CHESTNUT STREET
CHICAGO, ILLINOIS 60610

ADMIRAL CORPORATION
1191 MERCHANDISE MART
CHICAGO, ILLINOIS 60654

AEROJET GENERAL CORPORATION
DOCUMENTARY FILM SERVICES
SACRAMENTO, CALIFORNIA 95809

ALLEND'OR PRODUCTIONS
3449 CAHUENGA BOULEVARD, WEST
HOLLYWOOD, CALIFORNIA 90028

AMERICAN MANAGEMENT ASSOCIATION, INC.
FILM DEPARTMENT
AMERICAN MANAGEMENT ASSOCIATION BUILDING
135 WEST 50TH STREET
NEW YORK, NEW YORK 10020

PHONE. AREA CODE 212, 556-8238 OR 556-8316

RENTAL FEES
  INDIVIDUAL FILMS - $60.00-NONMEMBERS - $50.00-MEMBERS 7DAYS
  FILM SERIES - $300.00-NONMEMBER - $250.00-MEMBER 2 WEEKS
  URWICK LECTURES - $75.00-NONMEMBER - $90.00-MEMBER FILM
  URWICK LECTURES - $475-NONMEMBERS - $600-MEMBERS SERIES
  EDUCATIONAL INSTITUTIONS - SPECIAL RATES

MAKE RETURN SHIPMENT BY PARCEL POST
LATE RETURNS - $10.00 PER DAY
CANCELLATIONS AFTER SHIPMENT - REGULAR FEE

ARGONNE NATIONAL LABORATORY
DIVISION OF PUBLIC INFORMATION
U.S. ATOMIC ENERGY COMMISSION
WASHINGTON, D.C. 20545

ASSOCIATION FILMS, INC.
BROAD AT ELM
RIDGEFIELD, NEW JERSEY 07657

RENTAL FEES
  1 DAY - LISTED FEE
  ADDITIONAL DAYS - .5 LISTED FEE
  7 DAYS - 2.5 LISTED FEE
  SCHOOL WEEK - 2 LISTED FEE

RETURN TRANSPORTATION CHARGES PAID BY USER
OUTGOING TRANSPORTATION PAID BY USER AS REQUIRED
INSURANCE FEE OF $.10 TO $.20 PER SHIPMENT
RETURN FILMS IMMEDIATELY AFTER LAST SCHEDULED SHOWING
CANCELLATION AFTER 1 WEEK PRIOR TO SHOWING - REGULAR FEE

AUTONETICS DIVISION
PUBLIC RELATIONS DEPARTMENT
3370 MIRALOMA
ANAHEIM, CALIFORNIA 92803

BANK OF AMERICA
TRAINING SERVICES SECTION
1 SOUTH VAN NESS
SAN FRANCISCO, CALIFORNIA 94102

BELL TELEPHONE LABORATORIES, INC.
463 WEST STREET
NEW YORK, NEW YORK 10014

BENDIX CORPORATION
INDUSTRIAL CONTROLS DIVISION
FISHER BUILDING
DETROIT, MICHIGAN 48200

BOEING COMPANY
BOX 3707
SEATTLE, WASHINGTON 98100

BRAY STUDIOS, INC.
729 SEVENTH AVENUE
NEW YORK, NEW YORK 10019

BRIGHAM YOUNG UNIVERSITY
DEPT. OF AUDIOVISUAL COMMUNICATION
ATTN BOOKING CLERK
PROVO, UTAH 84601

PHONE. AREA CODE 801, 374-1211 EXT. 2713

RENTAL FEES
  1-3 DAYS - 1ST LISTED FEE
  5 DAYS - 2ND LISTED FEE

RETURN TRANSPORTATION PAID BY USER
USER RESPONSIBLE FOR LOSS OR DAMAGE WHILE IN POSSESSION
RETURN FILMS DAY AFTER USE
LATE RETURNS - $1.25 PER DAY
DO NOT REWIND FILMS
CANCELLATIONS AFTER 3 DAYS BEFORE SHIPMENT - REGULAR FEE
APPROVAL OF COPYRIGHT OWNER NECESSARY FOR TV SHOWING
ADMISSION FEES MAY NOT BE CHARGED FOR SHOWINGS

BURROUGHS CORPORATION
SECOND AVENUE AT BURROUGHS
DETROIT, MICHIGAN 48202

BUSINESS EDUCATION FILMS
5113 16TH AVENUE
BROOKLYN, NEW YORK 11204

PHONE. AREA CODE 212, 851-8090

RENTAL FEES
  1 DAY - LISTED FEE
  2 DAYS - 1.5 LISTED FEE
  3-5 DAYS - 2 LISTED FEE

TRANSPORTATION CHARGES BOTH WAYS PAID BY USER
RETURN BY PARCEL POST
FILMS INSURED DURING PROJECTION - $.10 FEE PAID BY USER
RETURN FILMS DAY FOLLOWING USE
LATE RETURNS - LISTED FEE PER DAY
CANCELLATIONS AFTER SHIPPING DATE - REGULAR FEE

BYRON, INC.
1226 WISCONSIN AVENUE, N.W.
WASHINGTON, D.C. 20007

CAMPUS FILM PRODUCTIONS, INC.
20 EAST 46TH STREET
NEW YORK, NEW YORK 10017

CAROUSEL FILMS, INC.
1501 BROADWAY
NEW YORK, NEW YORK 10036

CHARLES EAMES PRODUCTIONS
901 WASHINGTON BOULEVARD
VENICE, CALIFORNIA 90201

CHRYSLER CORPORATION
343 MASSACHUSETTS AVENUE
DETROIT, MICHIGAN 48203

CLASSROOM FILM DISTRIBUTORS
5620 HOLLYWOOD BOULEVARD
HOLLYWOOD, CALIFORNIA 90028

COLOR SERVICE, INC.
115 WEST 45TH STREET
NEW YORK, NEW YORK 10036

COLORADO STATE COLLEGE
INSTRUCTIONAL MATERIALS CENTER
ATTN. BOOKING CLERK
GREELEY, COLORADO 80631

PHONE. AREA CODE 303, 351-3093

RENTAL FEES
  1-3 DAYS - 1ST LISTED FEE
  5 DAYS - 2ND LISTED FEE

RETURN TRANSPORTATION PAID BY USER
USER RESPONSIBLE FOR LOSS OR DAMAGE WHILE IN POSSESSION
RETURN FILMS DAY AFTER USE
LATE RETURNS - $1.25 PER DAY
DO NOT REWIND FILMS
CANCELLATIONS AFTER 3 DAYS BEFORE SHIPMENT - REGULAR FEE
APPROVAL OF COPYRIGHT OWNER NECESSARY FOR TV SHOWING
ADMISSION FEES MAY NOT BE CHARGED FOR SHOWINGS

CONTEMPORARY FILMS, INC.
267 WEST 25TH STREET
NEW YORK, NEW YORK 10001

DEVRY TECHNICAL INSTITUTE
FILM SERVICE DEPARTMENT
4141 DELMOUNT AVENUE
CHICAGO, ILLINOIS 60641

RESERVATIONS THROUGH FIELD REPRESENTATIVES

DPD PROMOTIONAL SERVICES
WHITE PLAINS, NEW YORK 10600

EDITORIAL FILMS, INC.
10 EAST 40TH STREET
NEW YORK, NEW YORK 10016

EDUCATIONAL TESTING SERVICE
20 NASSAU STREET
PRINCETON, NEW JERSEY 08540

ELECTRONIC ASSOCIATES, INC.
LONG BRANCH AND NABERAL AVENUE
LONG BRANCH, NEW JERSEY 07740

ELECTRONIC DIVISION
GENERAL DYNAMICS CORPORATION
SAN DIEGO, CALIFORNIA 92100

  CONTACT LOCAL OFFICE

ELECTRONIC SYSTEMS LABORATORY
MASS. INSTITUTE OF TECHNOLOGY
BUILDING 32
CAMBRIDGE, MASSACHUSETTS 02139

NO RENTAL FEE

LOAN PERIOD - 2 WEEKS
RETURN FILMS AIR MAIL PARCEL POST, SPECIAL HANDLING
INSURE FILMS FOR $50.00 DURING RETURN TRANSIT

FILM ENTERPRISES, INC.
222 EAST 46TH STREET
NEW YORK, NEW YORK 10017

FILMTRONICS LABS
231 WEST 54TH STREET
NEW YORK, NEW YORK 10019

FORTUNE FILMS
FORTUNE MAGAZINE
ROCKEFELLER CENTER
NEW YORK, NEW YORK 10020

NO RENTAL FEE

RETURN TRANSPORTATION CHARGES PAID BY USER
RETURN FILMS PROMPTLY

GENERAL ELECTRIC COMPANY
FPD TECHNICAL INFORMATION CENTER
BLDG. 700 - N-32
CINCINNATI, OHIO 45215

NO RENTAL FEE

GOTHAM FILM SERVICE
ROOM 309
639 NINTH AVENUE
NEW YORK, NEW YORK 10036

HAMILTON FILM SERVICE
245 WEST 55TH STREET
NEW YORK, NEW YORK 10019

PHONE. AREA CODE 212, 757-4580

RENTAL FEES
  1 DAY - LISTED FEE
  ADDITIONAL DAYS - .5 LISTED FEE

HENRY STRAUSS PRODUCTIONS
31 WEST 53RD STREET
NEW YORK, NEW YORK 10019

HOLLYWOOD ANIMATORS, INC.
7401 SUNSET BOULEVARD
HOLLYWOOD, CALIFORNIA 90028

HOTCHKISS COLORFILM PRODUCTIONS
6739 MITCHELL AVENUE
ARLINGTON, CALIFORNIA 95521

HUGHES AIRCRAFT COMPANY
PUBLIC RELATIONS AND ADVERTISING
MAIL STATION 13
BUILDING 114
P.O. BOX 90515
LOS ANGELES, CALIFORNIA 90000

IBM

FILMS OBTAINED THROUGH LOCAL IBM OFFICES
NO RENTAL FEE

RETURN POSTAGE PAID BY USER
RETURN FILMS PROMPTLY
INSURE BW FILMS FOR $20/10 MIN. RUNNING TIME WHEN RETURNING
INSURE CR FILMS FOR $50/10 MIN. RUNNING TIME WHEN RETURNING

IDEAL PICTURES
616 SOUTH FIFTH STREET
LOUISVILLE, KENTUCKY 40202

INDIANA UNIVERSITY
AUDIO-VISUAL CENTER
BLOOMINGTON, INDIANA 47405

RENTAL FEES
 1-5 DAYS LISTED FEES

RETURN TRANSPORTATION PAID BY USER
DO NOT REWIND FILMS

INDUSTRIAL EDUCATION FILMS, INC.
195 NASSAU STREET
PRINCETON, NEW JERSEY 08540

INSTRUMENT SOCIETY OF AMERICA
PENN-SHEARTON HOTEL
530 WILLIAM PENN PLACE
PITTSBURG, PENNSYLVANIA 15219

INTERNATIONAL FILM BUREAU, INC.
332 SOUTH MICHIGAN AVENUE
CHICAGO, ILLINOIS 60604

JOHN COLBURN ASSOCIATES, INC.
1122 CENTRAL AVENUE
WILMETTE, ILLINOIS 60091

JOHN SUTHERLAND PRODUCTIONS, INC.
201 NORTH OCCIDENTAL BOULEVARD
LOS ANGELES, CALIFORNIA 90026

LOCKHEED MISSILE AND SPACE COMPANY
SUNNYVALE, CALIFORNIA 94086

MANAGEMENT SYSTEMS CORPORATION
2043 WESTCLIFF DRIVE
NEWPORT BEACH, CALIFORNIA 92660

MARTIN COMPANY
SPACE SYSTEMS DIVISION
BALTIMORE, MARYLAND 21200

MCGRAW-HILL BOOK COMPANY
TEXT-FILM DEPARTMENT
330 WEST 42ND STREET
NEW YORK, NEW YORK 10036

MERIT PRODUCTION OF CALIFORNIA
10044 BURNET AVENUE
SAN FERNANDO, CALIFORNIA 91343

MICHIGAN STATE UNIVERSITY
AUDIO-VISUAL CENTER
A-3 SOUTH CAMPUS
EAST LANSING, MICHIGAN 48823

PHONE. AREA CODE 517, 355-9623

RENTAL FEES
 3 DAYS - LISTED FEE
 4-5 DAYS - 1.4 LISTED FEE
 6-7 DAYS - 1.7 LISTED FEE
 8-10 DAYS - 2.0 LISTED FEE
 ADDITONAL SCHOOL WEEKS - .6 THE 4-5 FEE

TRANSPORTATION CHARGES BOTH WAYS PAID BY USER
RETURN FILMS ON SCHEDULED RETURN DATE
CHARGE MADE FOR LATE RETURNS
DO NOT REWIND FILMS
APPROVAL OF COPYRIGHT OWNER NECESSARY FOR SHOWING ON TV
ADMISSION FEES MAY NOT BE CHARGED FOR SHOWINGS

MINNESOTA MINING AND MANUFACTURING COMPANY
2501 HUDSON ROAD
ST. PAUL, MINNESOTA 55119

MOTION PICTURES
IBM
DEPARTMENT 906
OWEGO, NEW YORK 13827

MOVIELAB, INC.
619 WEST 54TH STREET
NEW YORK, NEW YORK 10019

N.E.T. FILM SERVICE
AUDIO-VISUAL CENTER
INDIANA UNIVERSITY
BLOOMINGTON, INDIANA 47401

NASA
OFFICE CF EDUCATIONAL PROGRAMS AND SERVICES
WASHINGTON, D.C. 20546

TRANSPORTATION CHARGES BOTH WAYS PAID BY USER
MAKE RETURN SHIPMENTS BY PARCEL POST
FILMS INSURED DURING USE AND IN TRANSIT
RETURN FILMS DAY FOLLOWING USE
APPROVAL OF DISTRIBUTOR NECESSARY TO SHOW FILMS ON TV

NATIONAL ASSOCIATION OF MANUFACTURERS
2 EAST 48TH STREET
NEW YORK, NEW YORK 10017

PICTORIAL PRESENTATION OF AMERICA, INC.
729 SEVENTH AVENUE
NEW YORK, NEW YORK 10019

NATIONAL CASH REGISTER COMPANY
AUDIO-VISUAL SERVICES
MARKETING SERVICES DEPARTMENT
DAYTON, OHIO 45409

NO RENTAL FEE

PRECISION FILM LABORATORIES, INC.
21 WEST 46TH STREET
NEW YORK, NEW YORK 10036

NATIONAL EDUCATIONAL TELEVISION
10 COLUMBUS CIRCLE
NEW YORK, NEW YORK 10019

PURDUE UNIVERSITY
AUDIO-VISUAL CENTER
LAFAYETTE, INDIANA 47901

NATIONAL FILM BOARD OF CANADA
SUITE 819
680 FIFTH AVENUE
NEW YORK, NEW YORK 10019

RAND CORPORATION
1700 MAIN STREET
SANTA MCNICA, CALIFORNIA 90401

NO RENTAL FEE

RETURN POSTAGE BY USER

NEW YORK CITY COLLEGE
FILM RENTAL SERVICE
AUDIO-VISUAL CENTER
17 LEXINGTON AVENUE
NEW YORK, NEW YORK 10010

PHONE. AREA CODE 212, 673-7700 EXT. 34 OR 35

RENTAL FEES
  1 DAY - LISTED FEE
  2 DAYS - 1.5 LISTED FEE
  3 DAYS - 2 LISTED FEE
  4-7 DAYS - 3 LISTED FEE

TRANSPORTATION CHARGES BOTH WAYS PAID BY USER
INSURE FILMS DURING RETURN TRANSIT
USER RESPONSIBLE FOR LOSS OR DAMAGE DURING POSSESSION
RETURN FILMS ON DATE INDICATED IN CONFIRMATION
CHARGE MADE FOR LATE RETURNS
FILMS MAY NOT BE SHOWN ON TV
ADMISSION FEES MAY NOT BE CHARGED FOR SHOWINGS

RAPHAEL WOLFF STUDIOS, INC.
1714 N. WILTON PLACE
HOLLYWOOD, CALIFORNIA 90028

RCA
ELECTRONIC DATA PROCESSING
CAMDEN, NEW JERSEY 08101

STATE UNIVERSITY OF IOWA
BUREAU OF AUDIO-VISUAL INSTRUCTION
EXTENSION DIVISION
IOWA CITY, IOWA 52240

PHONE. AREA CODE 319, 338-0511 EXT. 2671

FILMS SCHEDULED FOR 3 DAYS USE
RENTAL FEES
  3 DAYS - LISTED FEE
  4 DAYS-1 WEEK - LISTED FEE + $.50/400 FT. COLOR + $.60/400
  ADDITIONAL WEEKS - SAME AS FIRST WEEK

TRANSPORTATION CHARGES BOTH WAYS PAID BY USER
FILMS INSURED - $.10 FEE PAID BY USER
CANCELLATION AFTER SHIPPING DATE - REGULAR FEE
APPROVAL OF COPYRIGHT OWNER NECESSARY FOR SHOWING ON TV
ADMISSION FEES MAY NOT BE CHARGED FOR SHOWINGS

NEWSFILM, USA
ROOM 1527
250 WEST 57TH STREET
NEW YORK, NEW YORK 10019

ON FILMS, INC.
33 WITHERSPOON STREET
PRINCETON, NEW JERSEY 08540

STROMBERG-CARLSON CORPORATION
100 CARLSON ROAD
ROCHESTER, NEW YORK 14603

ORANGE COAST COLLEGE
COSTA MESA, CALIFORNIA 92626

SYRACUSE UNIVERSITY
EDUCATIONAL FILM LIBRARY
COLLENDALE CAMPUS D-7
SYRACUSE, NEW YORK 13210

PENNSYLVANIA STATE UNIVERSITY
AUDIO-VISUAL AIDS LIBRARY
UNIVERSITY PARK, PENNSYLVANIA 16802

RENTAL FEES
  1 DAY - LISTED FEE
  ADDITIONAL DAYS - .5 LISTED FEE
  1 WEEK - 3 LISTED FEE

PHONE. 315, 475-7763, OR 476-5571 EXT. 2452 OR 2453

FILMS SCHEDULED FOR 2 DAYS USE

RENTAL FEES
  1 SCHOOL WEEK - LISTED FEE
  2 SCHOOL WEEKS - 1.5 LISTED FEE
  3 SCHOOL WEEKS - 2 LISTED FEE

RETURN POSTAGE PAID BY USER
FILMS ARE INSURED IN TRANSIT
USER RESPONSIBLE FOR LOSS OR DAMAGE DURING POSSESSION
RETURN FILMS ON DATE INDICATED ON RETURN LABEL
LATE RETURNS - $1.00 PER DAY
DO NOT REWIND FILMS
CANCELLATIONS AFTER 14 DAYS PRIOR TO USE DATE - REGULAR FEE
APPROVAL OF PRODUCER NECESSARY FOR SHOWING ON TV

SYSTEM DEVELOPMENT CORPORATION
VISUAL ARTS SERVICES
2500 COLORADO AVENUE
SANTA MONICA, CALIFORNIA 90406

NO RENTAL FEE

LOAN PERIOD - 2 WEEKS
RETURN TRANSPORTATION PAID BY USER

THE ASSOCIATED STUDENT BOOK STORE
UNIVERSITY OF CALIFORNIA
DAVIS, CALIFORNIA 95616

TRAINING FILMS, INC.
150 WEST 54TH STREET
NEW YORK, NEW YORK 10019

U. S. ARMY
AUDIO-VISUAL COMMUNICATION CENTER
FORT GEORGE MEADE, MARYLAND 20755

NO RENTAL FEE

RETURN TRANSPORTATION CHARGE PAID BY USER
RETURN FILMS PROMPTLY
MAKE LOAN REQUEST 15 DAYS BEFORE USE
DO NOT REWIND FILMS

U.S. DEPARTMENT OF AGRICULTURE
14 STREET AT INDEPENDENCE AVENUE SW
WASHINGTON, D.C. 20250

PHONE. AREA CODE 202, 737-4142

U.S. INDUSTRIES
250 PARK AVENUE
NEW YORK, NEW YORK 10017

U.S. INTERNAL REVENUE SERVICE
12 STREET AND CONSTITUTION AVENUE NW
WASHINGTON, D.C. 20224

PHONE. AREA CODE 202, 783-8400

U.S. NAVY
ASSISTANT FOR PUBLIC INFORMATION
FIFTH NAVAL DISTRICT
BUILDING N-26, ROOM 105
NORFOLK, VIRGINIA 23511

NO RENTAL FEE

RETURN POSTAGE PAID BY USER
RETURN FILM WITHIN 48 HOURS AFTER USE
USE FILMS FOR EDUCATIONAL PURPOSES ONLY
APPROVAL NECESSARY FOR TV SHOWING

U.S. OFFICE OF EDUCATION
330 INDEPENDENCE AVENUE SW
WASHINGTON, D.C. 20201

PHONE. AREA CODE 202, 96 -1110

U.S.A.F. FILM LIBRARY CENTER
8900 SOUTH BROADWAY
ST. LOUIS, MISSOURI 63125

UNION CARBIDE NUCLEAR COMPANY
INDUSTRIAL RELATIONS DIVISION
P.O. BOX 1223
PADUCAH, KENTUCKY 42001

UNITED CHURCH OF CHRIST
BUREAU OF AUDIO-VISUALS
1501 RACE STREET
PHILADELPHIA, PENNSYLVANIA 19102

UNIVAC DIVISION
SPERRY RAND CORPORATION
FILM LIBRARY
1290 AVENUE OF AMERICAS
NEW YORK, NEW YORK 10019

  ALSO CONTACT BRANCH OFFICES

UNIVERSITY OF CALIFORNIA
EXTENTION MEDIA CENTER
2223 FULTON STREET
BERKELEY, CALIFORNIA 94720

PHONE. AREA CODE 415, 845-6000 EXT. 4106

RENTAL FEES
  1 DAY - LISTED FEE
  ADDITIONAL DAYS - .5 LISTED FEE

TRANSPORTATION CHARGES BOTH WAYS PAID BY USER
INSURE FILMS DURING RETURN TRANSIT
USER RESPONSIBLE FOR LOSS OR DAMAGE DURING POSSESSION
RETURN FILMS ON DATE INDICATED IN CONFIRMATION
LATE RETURNS - LISTED FEE PER DAY
CANCELLATION AFTER PACKAGING FOR SHIPMENT - REGULAR FEE
APPROVAL OF SALES-DISTRIBUTOR NECESSARY FOR TV SHOWING
FILMS MAY NOT BE USED FOR PROGRAMS TO OBTAIN PROFIT OR FUNDS

UNIVERSITY OF COLORADO
BUREAU OF AUDIOVISUAL INSTRUCTION
ATTN. BOOKING CLERK
BOULDER, COLORADO 80304

PHONE. AREA CODE 303, 443-2211 EXT. 7341

RENTAL FEES
  1-3 DAYS - 1ST LISTED FEE
  5 DAYS - 2ND LISTED FEE

RETURN TRANSPORTATION PAID BY USER
USER RESPONSIBLE FOR LOSS OR DAMAGE WHILE IN POSSESSION
RETURN FILMS DAY AFTER USE
LATE RETURNS - $1.25 PER DAY
DO NOT REWIND FILMS
CANCELLATIONS AFTER 3 DAYS BEFORE SHIPMENT - REGULAR FEE
APPROVAL OF COPYRIGHT OWNER NECESSARY FOR TV SHOWING
ADMISSION FEES MAY NOT BE CHARGED FOR SHOWINGS

UNIVERSITY OF GEORGIA
FILM LIBRARY
CENTER FOR CONTINUING EDUCATION
ATHENS, GEORGIA 30602

PHONE. AREA CODE 404, 543-2511 EXT. 579

RENTAL FEES
 1 DAY - LISTED FEE
 ADDITIONAL DAYS - .5 LISTED FEE
 1 WEEK - 2 LISTED FEE

FEE OF $.35 FOR FORWARD POSTAGE
RETURN POSTAGE PAID BY USER
FILMS NOT INSURED
USER RESPONSIBLE FOR LOSS OR DAMAGE DURING POSSESSION
RETURN FILMS DAY FOLLOWING USE
LATE RETURNS - LISTED FEE PER DAY
DO NOT REWIND FILMS
CANCELLATION AFTER SHIPMENT - REGULAR CHARGES
ADMISSION FEES MAY NOT BE CHARGED FOR SHOWINGS

UNIVERSITY OF KENTUCKY
AUDIO-VISUAL SERVICES
REYNOLDS BUILDING
LEXINGTON, KENTUCKY 40506

PHONE. AREA CODE 606, 252-2200 EXT. 2755

RENTAL FEES
 1 DAY - LISTED FEE
 2-3 DAYS - 1.5 LISTED FEE
 1 WEEK - 2 LISTED FEE

FORWARD TRANSPORTATION CHARGES FOR OUT OF STATE USERS
 $.50 PER REEL BLACK AND WHITE, $1.00 PER REEL COLOR
RETURN TRANSPORTATION PAID BY USER
FILMS NOT INSURED
USER RESPONSIBLE FOR DAMAGE OR LOSS AFTER FIRST OCCURRENCE
RETURN FILMS DAY AFTER USE
LATE RETURNS - $.50 PER DAY
DO NOT REWIND FILMS
CANCELLATIONS AFTER 1 WEEK PRIOR TO USE DATE - REGULAR FEE
APPROVAL OF COPYRIGHT OWNER NECESSARY FOR SHOWING ON TV
ADMISSION FEES MAY NOT BE CHARGED FOR SHOWINGS

UNIVERSITY OF MICHIGAN
AUDIO-VISUAL EDUCATION CENTER
720 E. HURON STREET, FRIEZE BUILDING
ANN ARBOR, MICHIGAN 48104

PHONE, AREA CODE 313, 663-1511, EXT. 2664

RENTAL FEES
 3 DAYS - LISTED FEE
 4-5 DAYS - 1.4 LISTED FEE
 6-7 DAYS - 1.7 LISTED FEE
 8-10 DAYS - 2.0 LISTED FEE
 ADDITIONAL SCHOOL WEEKS - .6 THE 4-5 FEE

TRANSPORTATION CHARGES BOTH WAYS PAID BY USER
RETURN FILMS ON SCHEDULED RETURN DATE
CHARGE MADE FOR LATE RETURNS
DO NOT REWIND FILMS
APPROVAL OF COPYRIGHT OWNER NECESSARY FOR SHOWING ON TV
ADMISSION FEES MAY NOT BE CHARGED FOR SHOWINGS

UNIVERSITY OF NEVADA
AUDIOVISUAL COMMUNICATION CENTER
ATTN. BOOKING CLERK
RENO, NEVADO 89507

PHONE. AREA CODE 702, 323-2081 EXT. 252

RENTAL FEES
 1-3 DAYS - 1ST LISTED FEE
 5 DAYS - 2ND LISTED FEE

RETURN TRANSPORTATION PAID BY USER
USER RESPONSIBLE FOR LOSS OR DAMAGE WHILE IN POSSESSION
RETURN FILMS DAY AFTER USE
LATE RETURNS - $1.25 PER DAY
DO NOT REWIND FILMS
CANCELLATION AFTER 3 DAYS BEFORE SHIPMENT - REGULAR FEE
APPROVAL OF COPYRIGHT OWNER NECESSARY FOR TV SHOWING
ADMISSION FEES MAY NOT BE CHARGED FOR SHOWINGS

UNIVERSITY OF SOUTHERN CALIFORNIA
LOS ANGELES, CALIFORNIA 90000

UNIVERSITY OF UTAH
AUDIOVISUAL BUREAU
MILTON BENNION HALL 207
SALT LAKE CITY, UTAH 84110

PHONE. AREA CODE 801, 322-6112

RENTAL FEES
 1-3 DAYS - 1ST LISTED FEE
 5 DAYS -2ND LISTED FEE

RETURN TRANSPORTATION PAID BY USER
USER RESPONSIBLE FOR LOSS OR DAMAGE WHILE IN POSSESSION
RETURN FILMS DAY AFTER USE
LATE RETURNS - $1.25 PER DAY
DO NOT REWIND FILMS
CANCELLATIONS AFTER 3 DAYS BEFORE SHIPMENT - REGULAR FEE
APPROVAL OF COPYRIGHT OWNER NECESSARY FOR TV SHOWING
ADMISSION FEES MAY NOT BE CHARGED FOR SHOWINGS

UNIVERSITY OF WASHINGTON
AUDIO-VISUAL SERVICE
LEWIS HALL
SEATTLE, WASHINGTON 98100

UNIVERSITY OF WYOMING
AUDIOVISUAL SERVICES
ATTN. BOOKING CLERK
LARAMIE, WYOMING 82070

PHONE. AREA CODE 307, 745-8511 EXT. 270

RENTAL FEES
 1-3 DAYS - 1ST LISTED FEE
 5 DAYS -2ND LISTED FEE

RETURN TRANSPORTATION PAID BY USER
USER RESPONSIBLE FOR LOSS OR DAMAGE WHILE IN POSSESSION
RETURN FILMS DAY AFTER USE
LATE RETURNS - $1.25 PER DAY
DO NOT REWIND FILMS
CANCELLATION AFTER 3 DAYS BEFORE SHIPMENT - REGULAR FEE
APPROVAL OF COPYRIGHT OWNER NECESSARY FOR TV SHOWING
ADMISSION FEES MAY NOT BE CHARGED FOR SHOWINGS

WESTERN ELECTRIC

 CONTACT LOCAL BUSINESS OFFICE OF TELEPHONE COMPANY

www.ingramcontent.com/pod-product-compliance
Lightning Source LLC
Chambersburg PA
CBHW080605060326
40689CB00021B/4941